TRAILBLAZERS

The Life, Leadership and
Legacy of Achievers

RAAM ANAND et. al.

STARDOM BOOKS

www.StardomBooks.com

STARDOM BOOKS
112 Bordeaux Ct.
Coppell, TX 75019, USA

FIRST EDITION FEBRUARY 2025

STARDOM BOOKS, LLC.
112 Bordeaux Ct. Coppell, TX 75019, USA

www.stardombooks.com

Stardom Books, United States
Stardom Alliance, India

The author and publishers have made all reasonable efforts to contact copyright holders for permission and apologize for any omissions or errors in the form of credits given. Corrections may be made to future editions.

TRAILBLAZERS / The Life, Leadership and Legacy of Achievers

Stardom Alliance

p. 174

cm. 13.97 X 21.59

Category:
BUS046000 - Business & Economics : Motivational
BUS025000 - Business & Economics : Entrepreneurship
SEL021000 - Self-Help : Motivational & Inspirational

ISBN: 978-1-957456-69-0

DEDICATION

This book is dedicated to all those amazing souls who dug their heels into the ground and persevered on the roads not taken, creating their own journey in life. Surviving the struggles and obstacles that no one else has dared brave before—there is no better name for them than "Trailblazers."

DISCLAIMER

The views, opinions and information presented in this book are from the co-authors of the publication. The publisher does not endorse or subscribe to the information; reader discretion is solicited.

This book is designed to provide information on how each one of the co-authors did what they did, as their own personal narrative. It is sold with the understanding that neither the co-authors nor the publisher is engaged in rendering legal, accounting or other professional services. If legal or other professional advice is warranted, the services of an appropriate professional should be sought. Also, this book cannot be an exhaustive and complete presentation on the topics within the book. While every effort has been made to make the information presented here as complete and accurate as possible, it may contain errors, omissions or information that was accurate as of its publication but subsequently has become outdated by marketplace or industry changes or conditions, new laws or regulations, or other circumstances.

Neither the co-authors nor the publisher accepts any liability or responsibility to any person or entity with respect to any loss or damage alleged to have been caused, directly or indirectly, by the information, ideas, opinions or other content in this book. If you do not agree to these terms, you should immediately return this book for full refund.

NOTE FROM THE PUBLISHER

It was a great pleasure to work with all the CO-AUTHORS of this book to bring out their stories, perspectives, and insights on how they did what they did. Each one of them have gone through their own struggles, overcome challenges successfully steered and their businesses and careers into becoming a well-known names in their respective industries. Through this publication, I wanted to bring out their views so that you, the reader, can benefit and get inspired by their achievements. The experts were specifically asked to share how they did what they did and their message to the world. So, here it is, not just for your reading pleasure but also as a reference guide to help you shorten the learning curve and outshine your own personal endeavors. As you are going to learn by reading from the contributors of this book, you will understand that all of them have one common thing to say… TAKE ACTION. Go ahead, read the book, take action and bring about a positive difference in your life, business and career – today!

RAAM ANAND, PUBLISHER.

CONTENTS

ACKNOWLEDGMENTS

Often, you've come across this section in a book, only to find
that the author has dedicated it to someone else, someone
unknown or non-existent. Not this time. I want to express
my gratitude to you, the reader, for your role in making this
book a success. Your decision to pick up this book and invest
your time in it is truly appreciated. I would be even more
grateful if you read the book and took action to further your
life and create a positive difference.

1

THE LIFE, LEADERSHIP AND LEGACY OF MURALI DHARAN

A TALE OF ENTREPRENEURIAL RESILIENCE

To be different is like being a radiant sunflower amidst a field of scarlet roses, standing tall with its golden vibrancy that refuses to be overshadowed. At first glance, such individuality might be intimidating and even lonesome. Yet, it does not imply doom and gloom; instead, it often opens a portal to a path less trodden, filled with potential and rewarding surprises. Standing out, after all, bestows upon you an unforgettable character, like a unique brushstroke on a canvas full of uniform hues. It morphs you into a singular melody in a symphony that echoes in the same key. Albert Einstein's profound wisdom served as my guiding beacon during such challenging times, his enlightening words being, "The person who follows the crowd will usually go no further than the crowd. The person who walks alone is likely to find himself in places no one has ever seen before."

I, Murali Dharan, did not want to follow any crowd. I wanted to build my own niche and would like to share my journey with all of you. To begin with, I did my schooling in different places as my father had a transferable job. I graduated from Bangalore. After that, I did my Masters in Coimbatore. After school, I joined my graduation in Chemistry, but my grandfather wanted me to do a professional degree. He pulled me into Bangalore and enrolled me at a private engineering college. After joining there, it really shook me because until I was 12, I was in an enclosed atmosphere with my parents. It was the first time my wings were opening because I had never even gone to a movie alone until I was 12.

I had a lot of friends in Bangalore, so I learned nearly four languages very quickly. After that, I took my TOEFL and GRE exams and got good scores. I was admitted to Oklahoma University but did not join because I did not get the scholarship. I did not want to tax my father then and didn't have the guts to do it. Later, I tried to do an MBA, which did not work out well. My father pushed me to do a post-graduation course. Once I finished college, I got my job on campus and started working in FRICK India, Delhi, and later, I shifted to Oman. Today, it has been nearly 25 years since I have been here, and I started my own company around 13 years ago. I have created one more company in India and Dubai.

In Oman, we started trading on HVAC equipment and are slowly turning ourselves into contractors and key solution providers. Trading and Contracting are two different ball games, whether in India or Oman, where we have just started becoming contractors because trading could be more fruitful/challenging, and there is also a change in the market requirement of having one point contact for an activity. In the last quarter of 2023, we started becoming contractors, and we are hopeful of getting bigger jobs. In Oman, we are trading and contracting. We have around 30 exclusive agencies for a month for the products, which are primarily associated with building services. We are contracting for the false ceilings and fit-outs along with the products. To make it more professional in our approach to the market, all my companies are ISO 9001 certified. In Oman, we have the three certifications we got: 9001, 14001, and 45001.

To be honest, it was not in my plan at all to start a business, but it happened. I came for a vacation to Muscat after winding up my job in Oman in 2010, and my friends said, "Let's start a business," and then we signed in. The critical part of my journey has been my supporters' mainly my friends and goodwill. When we started the company in 2010, we had a government policy that we should block 150 thousand riyals in the bank. Only then can you start an LLC company. I didn't have enough money back then, so I had to borrow money from my friends. The bank had given me a deadline of four days. I just informed my friends about this, and to my surprise, I got 160 thousand rials in the account before the deadline, over the required limit. That is how we started the journey, which was not planned but moved on well. From there, we have been picking up businesses, and by God's grace, we have got around 20 staff in Oman, 18 staff in Chennai, and a couple of staff in Dubai.

My father is a retired college professor and the joint director of education. As the son of a professor, I find it a different ball game altogether because they push you into an idealistic situation, which is far from reality. But having said that, we were never into the realm of business. There are people in our family doing business, but we were not into that. We are only the working side of it. But my father was a good support when I chatted with him about starting a business. Despite hailing from a middle-class family, my father was very supportive, and I found confidence. The confidence helped me not to be afraid to take that jump. I never wanted to slack off. My company's punchline was a "one stop solution". So, if a client wants anything regarding building services, we should have all the items under one umbrella. We tried to cover the complete spectrum; then, we wanted a one-stop solution for all the building services. That was the intention from day one. We started it in 2010, and it has been 13 years.

In my career, I worked only at three companies, firmly believing there is an opportunity to learn in every walk of life or job. In Oman, I worked for a trading company. My boss was Mr. George, and he had a small company with three people. It was very challenging because he was very tough, and the negotiations on all these matters were very tough and highly connected. He offered me the job and said, "I cannot give you the brand. But I can give you whatever salary you want." When I told my father that it was a great opportunity and that if it did not work out, I would come back to India. The whole world was against me, saying that I was taking the wrong step, but only my father supported me. But I have to give credit to Mr. George, who trusted his business on me, never interfered with my decisions and operations, and gave me a free hand. It gave me immense opportunities to learn and operate the company on my terms, and we managed to increase the turnover by ten times in six years. Right through my career, all my bosses, only three of them, Mr. Manmohan Singh, Mr. Ranjan, and Mr. George, had been my inspirations and always supported and trained me in building confidence and quality, which is the basis for running an organization. Without this, I would not have leaped from working in a community to business.

When I was planning to leave Oman in 2009, the trading company made 3 million turnovers with independent, autonomous departments. The most important thing we were doing was BMS (a control system for the complete building). You can do the full building controls from one place. We built up agencies and brought nearly thirty different products for them. We got an agency from Cylon Ireland for the building management system through a friend, Mr. John Cameron, in Mar 2011. We were maintaining all five palaces of Oman for the building management system—a very challenging and demanding activity, which we managed to achieve.

The transition from an employee to an entrepreneur never arose from doubts. The challenge was quite exciting but not depressing. During the journey, I had a few allies, too. My bosses were always good. First to start at Frick, India— It was Manmohan Singh. He was a very tough guy with a sharp tongue. Secondly, Mr. Malhotra shaped me too in my journey. Thirdly, George helped me develop confidence. He said, "Do whatever you want. It's okay Be it good or bad, everything is yours." He trusted me that I would not mess up anything and I would do great things. By God's grace, things have worked out well. Nobody can give that confidence to anyone. Today, while running a company myself, I cannot tell any employee to do whatever they please. Therefore, I am grateful for the opportunities I have received. All my bosses have been very supportive. Even now, all my bosses are in communicative terms.

I never had any technical challenges because I was not shy in asking people if I did not know something. My competitor was a very good acoustic engineer, Mr. Gaurav. I went down to Dubai and sat with him. I told him that I wanted to start this Acoustics department and might become a competitor. Since he is a good friend, he taught me a lot of basics about it. Like him, there were a lot of people who pushed me into it, and I was not shy to ask them. For I know that not everybody is perfect and not everybody is knowledgeable. Not everyone knows everything. Learning is a curve until you are dead.

When I started the company, my only goal was to have one umbrella covering the building services, solutions, and products; because I was a mechanical engineer, I did my Master's in Thermal. Therefore, air conditioning was in my blood. That itself is a colossal lifetime scope It is not going to entail. As of now, in the past 13 years, we have given a lot of leverage to add new products. For example, this year, we added new products because now sustainability and power saving is an important thing. It is very challenging to get the right products, which we were able to and also we created an excellent website, which now is the driving factor.

We introduced several new products, which is the first time anyone else has in the market. For example, we are finding an alternative solution for cooling air conditioning, it is adiabatic cooling. Therefore, without a compressor and gas, we can generate cooling only with water. With technology we can achieve this. We are working with companies from the Netherlands and India. In a building for operating, there are two major power expenses. One is power for the lighting part or the owner's power for the air conditioning or ventilation part. That is a significant thing in India; most of the companies nowadays are in that condition. Before that, it was all naturally ventilated. The power is now only in two major areas: lighting and air-conditioning. We have now introduced a lighting solution with solar tunnels from Europe, which will reduce the carbon footprint in the building. We are known for bringing new products. When the market has any issues, people usually call us to help them.

There is a massive area of growth because assets are building services. It is a statement covering all the sectors: civil, mechanical, air conditioning, electrical systems. It works for everything. In India, we try to add new products. Today, we feel a sense of satisfaction that we have achieved something. When you are giving salaries for, say forty to fifty people a month that puts you in a different spectrum. Even during the COVID-19 period, we paid the entire salary without reducing a single penny. That has been our thing, even though I don't know whether the staff is going to appreciate it, but we feel good about it. We have done that, as of today, we have never stopped the salaries and distributed on time. That is the biggest challenge because, with the market, there are a lot of issues with the cash flow. Therefore, we have to constantly keep working, adding new products, and adding new directions. For example, this false ceiling and drywall partitions as a contracting itself is a game to enter into that to improve the cash flow. At the end of the day, we have to keep the ball rolling and keep everybody paid.

If I had to give any advice to a budding entrepreneur, I would say that one should not start anything until they are sure or until they have that experience. There are a lot of college freshers who are starting a business. Now, having an idea for the company and running a business are two different things. Starting a business is possible, but maintaining the business and sustaining it is another ball game altogether. If you see the graph in India, there are a lot of startups, but after two years, most of them are barely flowing. Therefore, work in a line where you want to start. For example, if you want to create an IT company, then work at an IT company and not a big corporation. Learn the problems over there and switch to more prominent companies after you master the art of problem-solving.

When running a business, you are committed to your staff to pay the salary and other things. Therefore, you should be prepared to face the challenge first. For that preparation, you have to work with somebody to gain experience and then do it right. I remember there was a speech by Mr. Ratan Tata that when he was working, he was put on the floor to work so he knew the problem and how to solve it. He will learn how to solve the problem required for us to run a business because you need a solution to solve the issues.

I believe that the purpose of getting into a college is not just for you to read. The first is to give you training like coming to college on time, say 9 am. You have to sit there for hours, whether you like it or not, whether the teacher is boring or not, you have to spend that time in college. This sequence is what is going to help you in life. We may not use all that we read in college. I have never used calculus in my life. My Engineers use psychrometric charts, but I have never used them. The training you receive in college leads you to get into a habit or a sequence that is useful for your life. For example, getting up early and going to college is a challenge to start with. Therefore, this sequence, whether you like it or not, teaches you about discipline. During college, you learn how to prepare yourself for a job. Once you get the job, what you know and what you do will be different. In practical reality, it is different.

As an entrepreneur, when you have the guts to face the wrong things, you will also have the ability to find the solution. I would say I am a one-man team, but I take my staff along with me. Without my staff, I am nothing. In life, you have to be fair; you have to be clever but not cunning. Even today, I do not have to fix an appointment with the contracting company. I just say, "Can I come?" and they say yes. This is the relationship that has been developed over some time. We have been very open with people and helped them when they needed something. The transformation from India to Oman was vast; I was in a very close atmosphere. The change in life has kept me grounded and made me feel grateful for everything I have. Friends and families have been there for me and even fed me. I have been blessed with a lot of good people in my life. Everything happens for the good. Therefore, I move with the flow and embrace the randomness of life.

This journey was no stroll in the park. It was a relentless, grueling marathon that demanded the tenacity of a seasoned athlete. It wasn't an impulsive burst of courage that led me down this path, nor was the journey a soothing river cruise. It was a tumultuous ocean voyage, demanding an iron will and an unwavering spirit, much like an ancient mariner daring to face an unforgiving storm. Everything that I am today results from my father's enlightening teachings, his unwavering support, and his wisdom illuminating my path like a lighthouse guiding a ship through the stormy sea. During life's most challenging phases, you are placed in a crucible, the relentless furnace of adversity, which blisters away to reveal the genuine gold beneath. In this crucible, I found myself distinguishing between the wheat and the chaff, between true allies and mere masqueraders. The chorus of sympathetic onlookers, their condolences echoing like a mournful dirge, barely brushed past the resilient shield of my resolve.

MURALI DHARAN, CO-AUTHOR

An expert in engineering and project management, **Murali Dharan** has successfully led complex initiatives that blend innovation with precision execution. With a keen analytical mind and a commitment to excellence, he has been at the forefront of designing and implementing large-scale projects. Murali's work provides readers with a comprehensive understanding of project dynamics, equipping professionals with the tools to drive efficiency, quality, and strategic success in the engineering domain.

2

THE LIFE, LEADERSHIP AND LEGACY OF JOHN CHERIAN

FROM INCEPTION TO VICTORY: THE STORY OF ENPARADIGM

"Life is what happens when you have other plans."
-Bettina Arndt

We generally build several dreams during our teenage, hoping that we will grow up to become the person we dreamt we would become. But like Bettina Arndt rightly said, life is something that pops up while you're still busy crafting other plans. Codes and computers have been my playground ever since childhood. I worked my brain well enough to absorb all the nuances of computer language. The thing with programmers is when people talk in standard English, we communicate using codes. I could only imagine getting hired by some top IT company; nothing more, nothing less.

Although cerebrally advanced, I was never that typical bookworm kind of an individual. I was a happy-go-lucky guy with a keen interest in hands-on and practical things. I used to love learning interesting techniques related to computers. I was an introvert in school, but as I grew up, I realized I needed more friends and more fun. I could see everyone hanging out on weekends and having the best time of their lives, which naturally instilled a major FOMO in me. In no time, I made friends with a number of incredible people in college. I would say it was a sudden flip. It is never easy to transform from an introvert to an extrovert just like that. It did take me a lot of time and effort.

I come from a family where everyone believes in government jobs and services. There was not even a single person who owned a business. Business, in an average Indian family, is generally directly associated with loss of money. Little do they realize the coin has two sides. If one is a failure, certainly there is success and profit on the other side. Like any other Indian mother, my mom also wanted me to pursue the traditional path of finding a nice job after scoring well in college. Well, I won't blame her because that was what I had also planned for myself- to find a job as a programmer! I finished my undergrad in computer science with flying colors and started off my career as a programmer in a famous tech firm.

I was having a pretty good time with my colleagues and managers. However, I could also sense that I didn't fit perfectly inside the team, just like a puzzle with a little thicker edge that cannot squeeze itself into the picture despite being the right piece. My managers were truly supportive and sensible, but again, like I said, I had a constant urge to improve so many things within the organization. My brain, which was initially fully immersed and drowning in the world of computers, decided to come to the surface of the waters and take a panorama view of the business world. "well, should I move out of the company and start exploring and learning new things?", I asked myself. The answer was certainly a "yes," after which I joined IIMA to pursue a master's in business administration, which is a two-year course.

I knew that my parents, who were happy with the fact that I worked for an IT company, might find it difficult to digest, so I gave them a heads-up before joining college. That way, I knew they would get two long years to process this in their head.

When I joined the business school, I was exposed to many new business concepts and techniques that have the potential to be life changers. I even got an opportunity to attend an entrepreneurship motivation lecture by Prof. Sunil Handa, an IIMA alumnus and entrepreneur himself. He is truly a veteran with immense patience and expertise. We all had our own sets of doubts, and he ensured everything was cleared before the sessions ended.

IIMA was not the answer to my questions ever; rather, it presented me with a number of questions that have to be answered. Despite knowing I wanted to become an entrepreneur, I had no clue what business to start and which business model to follow. The problem with IIMA is that it doesn't give you one idea but thousands of them, making your brain extremely saturated with an ocean of options. Honestly, that was one major problem I had to face- lack of clarity! However, things soon changed for the good. It all started with a surprising opportunity—a chance to create a simulation for a business school competition, thanks to my friend Shankar, who roped me in along with a team of enthusiastic first-year students. None of us knew how to make a simulation, but fueled by determination, we spent countless nights—more than twenty— coding and fixing bugs until the very last moments when the participants were ready to dive into the game.

The nail-biting moments came when we tested the simulation engine to ensure it accurately reflected the decisions made by the players. Fortunately, our professors, Prof. Bibek and Prof. Arindam, who previously used simulations from Western providers, encouraged us by pointing out a potential market for these simulations. This is when I realized that I could consider starting a business by incorporating my knowledge in simulation.

Another major conflict I faced while I was in IIMA was that, ours was the first batch starting from which the institute decided to stop heavily flowing subsidized education. Such an unfortunate event, I should say; our fee was thrice the amount that our seniors had to pay. For several of us, it was indeed a challenge. Students had to apply for loans that were unheard of for public institutions back then. Those who applied for the loan were too worried, wondering how to pay off the debts.

However, opting for an MBA was indeed a great idea. The institute wasn't just a building but a place where I could see my passion unfolding. Colleges usually host meet-and-greet with famous authors and entrepreneurs, and I'm sure you must have had the opportunity to meet many eminent personalities while you were in college. The resource person doesn't necessarily have to be an external person. It can be someone from within the institution as well. I happened to hear an amazing lecture from one of our professors, Prof. Bibek, (one of the professors who helped us with the simulation) which was indeed an eye-opener.

I also had the opportunity to meet Prof. Sunil Handa, who provided us with a course on entrepreneurial motivation in the 2nd year, which hugely helped us learn more about becoming an entrepreneur. After coming across all these people and their lectures, I knew for sure that I should become an entrepreneur. One of my most favorite professors, Prof. (name) used to say you must be hungry and foolish at the same time in order to become a successful entrepreneur. Now, why "hungry" and "foolish"? Because the moment you are done with your masters degree, you won't have so many things to do immediately. You probably don't know what to do and where to go. You do need money, but you don't have any, and you aren't sure what to do next. That's the best time to start a business because, apparently, you don't have anything to lose. When you start working a full-time job, you may not have the guts to leave a well-paying job to invest in business. Or even if you think you can, you won't be able to due to pressure from every side. Once you start earning and spending, your responsibilities go up even before you realize it, and people start expecting a lot from you. Therefore, Prof. (name) says it is always better to start from zero.

Like a good student, I decided to obey my professors and started my dream business in a tiny room with just three chairs and our own laptops right after postgraduation. We spent one whole year inside that single hall. We hardly had to spend any money. We paid a rent amount of around a thousand rupees for the hall. A major portion of the money was spent only on food, and toward the end of the year, we figured out we had spent only around 70 to 75 thousand rupees altogether, which is not a huge amount considering the fact that we are talking about a year, not a month.

The only challenge we had to go through was the fact that two out of the three founders were still bearing the debt of their education. As I already said, IIM did make it a little harder for our batch by lifting the subsidizing policy. But again, we knew that to pay the EMIs, we had to have money, and to make money, it was absolutely necessary to kick-start the business and make it a success.

Now, if you are to ask me what kept us going forward, I still do not have a clear answer to it. But one thing we knew for sure- in business, it is either up or down. There is no in-between. You always need to aim at the up in order to be able to climb the ladder effectively. I knew how much I wanted to become an entrepreneur, and I was never ready to give up. When you are a person with ideas but can't execute them at your workplace, you should probably find a way out and create a space for yourself where your ideas will hold value.

When you work for a corporate company, you require approval from your seniors to make something happen within the organization, which is indeed tiring and disheartening. Every time I went up to someone to talk about something innovative, I was given a list of reasons as to why my plan didn't make sense to them, and obviously, it made me apprehensive and disappointed. I left the job to pursue an MBA to ensure that my opinions were valued. For me, it was an extremely exciting and rewarding journey where I could literally see that I was giving power to myself to fly better and higher after graduation. I could finally give myself ownership of things without external constraints. People generally climb the corporate ladder upwards to find success and earn well, and there are people from the IAS IPS background trying hard to get promoted to an ever higher position. Everything is normal and equally rewarding; the only thing is you need to have an idea of what you really want in life. Business, in my opinion, is the fastest way to grow without putting the blame on anybody else. Remember that you can seek influence and inspiration from the whole world.

Growing up, I saw my parents as strong influencers. They were two individuals with completely contradictory perspectives and thoughts. They never had the same opinion about anything. But, to me, that turned out to be a blessing because I always had options and knew the consequences of each and every action. For instance, hypothetically, if my dad thinks I should play cricket and my mom thinks I should practice football and I'm standing there totally confused, both of them explain or rather defend their points very well. So what about the confused child in between? I get two unique and interesting perspectives and can choose whichever suits me the best. It is always great to listen to one thing from two different perspectives and gain some idea than to proceed with one thing that randomly pops into your head without any clarity. You get two ways to deal with things. My mom was extremely religious, whereas my dad was an atheist. He had a happy-go-lucky approach towards everything. He digs down deep into the core concept of everything.

I still remember years ago, he taught me how a motorcycle works in simple and comprehendible language. The next week, our physics teacher taught us the same thing at school and made it sound extremely complicated. Unfortunately, the Indian education system has a habit of making everything look complex. However, Dad helped me break down every tiny concept so that I could learn it with ease.

He would disagree with things that he doesn't like without second thoughts. He doesn't support anything just because the rest of the people support the same. He always stood by his opinion. He never gets influenced by something somebody says. However, Mom, on the other hand, believed in institutions and beliefs. While Dad questioned things, Mom remained compliant.

Our parents come from a place where they only had Doordarshan to watch and an Ambassador car to commute. Yet they came so far in life to a point where they can adapt to any situation. Also, I should say that we belong to a lucky generation because we have somebody to teach us how to live through tough times, and to make things even better, we are witnessing first-hand the advancements that technology is bringing to our lives.

Both my parents, despite the changes and contradictions in opinions, were a team, and ever since, I started believing in Team Power, too. We can do a lot of things alone, but not everything! We do need people around us to support and guide us through everything. While my mom used to stick to rules and my father believed in questioning everything, their son turned out to be a proper blend of both. As I kick-started my start-up called En-Paradigm in 2008, I knew I had to come up with some rules so that my teammates could work together on it.

In my opinion, there have to be some rules for the basic things that exist within any company so that people can work on it by focusing on a singular goal; I mean, that way, we will all be on the same page. However, rules aren't everything that matters; we do have to keep an eye on our realities. EnParadigm is a company that focuses on corporate learning and development. We specialize in providing learning solutions specifically made for the corporate world. We provide simulation-based learning experiences, strategic management programs, leadership development, and other customized educational modules which ultimately aims at enhancing professional skills and business acumen within organizations. Since we were looking forward to provide services for a larger group of people, we had to be very careful with every step we took. My expectations and reality had a lot of contradictions, which I was obviously prepared for. It wasn't very glamorous initially, and I knew that it was never going to be easy.

Firstly, my startup did not have heavy investments. We started off from a humble hall with three chairs and desks, which we called our workstation. Gradually, when it started growing, I was able to hire more people to join the journey. But the difference between working in a corporate environment and working on your own business is that, in the former, you can go to your manager if you come across an issue that you cannot resolve; however, in the latter, you are the one leading the pack. A problem comes to you when nobody else can handle it. You need to be capable of taking it upon your shoulders and dealing with it. If it is something that you cannot figure out, you have to learn. Of course, you can approach your mentors, but there is only so much they can do to help you, considering the fact that they all come from different places. Yours could be a textile business, but if your mentor comes from a hotel business, your ideas would never align well. You may or may not take their advice, but if it doesn't work out for you, never blame the mentor.

Hard work and creating value are two different concepts. You may be a very hardworking individual, but it doesn't mean your customers will be happy with your so-called hard work. That is where value creation comes into the picture. Human beings remain students forever, right? In the process of learning, it is important to understand how to create value for your customers. As a business owner, I sometimes find the process of pricing difficult. Things might look expensive to the customer, and they might feel disappointed. I had to do something about it, and after spending some time on it, we, as a team, decided to provide services in a way that could create value for the customers. We still focus on customer satisfaction over revenue generation. But this is indeed a challenge faced by most entrepreneurs.

The thing about owning a business is that you will never face a shortage of work. You get to deal with different types of queries and problems and whatnot! However, resolving these problems and moving forward alone doesn't make your organization successful. As I said, our reality and the reality of our customers might be entirely different. They do align very rarely, but then, you cannot really sit and hope that they would be fine with everything you present them with. You must have the ability to empathize with them and provide them with exactly what they need. You need to make changes to some of your rules and iterations in order to make it convenient for the clients, especially when it comes to a large market. You may or may not win the heart of the client, but still, you must possess the ability to quickly make sensible changes to your rules to make them feel good.

What I have understood from my journey, which I would love to share with you, is that business usually looks like a one-way street in the beginning. The more you keep moving in the right direction, the more likely you are to come across closed doors. Never sit right in front of the closed door and cry your lungs out. Instead, go in search of open doors. The closed doors are what make you stronger. If you are very well determined, you never lose; you either learn or earn.

Starting off this journey has been a true source of strength. In the beginning, my aim was clear: rather than sitting back and hoping for change, I wanted to take the opportunity to create it myself. Kumar Veetrag and I shared a lifelong conviction in the importance of improved education, one that is both higher in quality and more directly applicable. It brings us immense happiness to know that each day, we are actively contributing to reshaping the landscape of corporate learning. This pursuit isn't just a passion; it's a commitment to enhancing the way we learn and grow.

Learning from Prof. Sunil Handa's course on entrepreneurial motivation in my second year was a game-changer. It opened my eyes to the world of entrepreneurship and provided invaluable insights into what it takes to thrive in this space. The network I built at IIMA turned out to be a treasure trove of support. Whenever we ventured into new cities for market analysis or sought feedback, there was always someone from the IIMA network ready to lend a hand. Prof. P Sutharshan, an alumnus and ex-director of ISRO, played a crucial role in those early days when our business was just starting out, and we had only a few employees beyond the founders. His guidance was priceless. The Presidents of various alumni chapters also stepped in, offering their mentorship and support.

As our business grew, we sought counsel from Prof. Ramesh Srinivasan and Prof. Rajan Narayanan, engaging them in regular monthly meetings as our sounding board. The help we received extended beyond these individuals; countless others contributed along the way. If I were to share advice with budding entrepreneurs, it would be this: don't hesitate to ask for help. In fact, be bold and shameless about it. Sometimes, pride can hold us back, but at the beginning stages, there's nothing to lose by seeking guidance and assistance. The support and wisdom gained from others have been instrumental in our journey, and I believe it's an essential part of every entrepreneur's path to success.

Initially, we were three co-founders, and our focus turned towards understanding the corporate education landscape. We wanted to find a niche that could compete effectively with prestigious business schools and other global brands in the field. Despite months of discussions with customers, clarity about their needs remained elusive. But instead of waiting for absolute certainty, we decided to take the leap and create simulations anyway.

Sometimes, waiting for absolute clarity isn't the key. Taking action, learning along the way, and being adaptable can lead to unexpected opportunities. Our journey into creating simulations might have started with uncertainty, but it taught us the value of taking bold steps even in the absence of complete clarity.

As we moved closer to our goals, the road got bumpy. After the initial couple of years, tensions brewed within the original team of co-founders. Kumar Veetrag, my co-founder, and I faced a tough time when one of our co-founders chose to part ways and pursue a different direction. Such splits among co-founders can often spell disaster for young companies. Therefore, it is important to ensure that all the founders are on the same page. It is great to have people with different ideas and opinions, but it is never healthy to have people with other life goals within your startup.

In the entrepreneurial journey, challenges persist as a constant companion. The ride is rarely steady; it swings between remarkable highs and daunting lows, leaving little room for autopilot moments. We ventured into multiple business ideas that failed to match our expectations in scaling up. We juggled huge loans, funds from friends and family, and equity from VCs. There were moments when we separated a business unit into a distinct company, with co-founders relocating and launching international subsidiaries. We teetered on the brink of financial depletion several times, even having to make the difficult decision of layoffs during the COVID era.

Our journey has been a spectrum—marked by periods of high burn and moments of significant cash generation, each business unit carrying its unique dynamics. Initially, assembling the right team was a puzzle. Now, I prioritize qualities like chemistry, complementarity, and competence when hiring. Every addition must seamlessly integrate into our existing structure in the short and medium term.

The glossy narratives in startup PR and VC funds paint a landscape of rocketing success, but the reality is more akin to a turbulent roller coaster ride. Maintaining emotional equilibrium amidst these fluctuations is crucial. Balancing highs and lows without letting emotions sway too far in either direction is vital. It's essential not to succumb to external pressures or unnecessary comparisons with others' journeys.

We experiment; some ventures flourish, while others falter. The key is to extract lessons and keep progressing. Movement signifies progress; as long as we keep moving, we're advancing toward our goals.

I don't believe in the concept of the "biggest goal." It is a journey that keeps going. It is very important to be goal-oriented and focused, but you have to enjoy the journey as well instead of only being overfocused on the goal. Focusing only on the goal is bound to bring misery when you can't achieve it and takes away all the great work that happened along the journey as well.

I keep podcasting about a lot of the lessons I have learned at enSights https://www.enparadigm.com/podcast - lessons about how to hire the right team, how to look for the right talent, how to look at things from a first principles perspective, how to navigate the early changes and manage founder relationships, etc. You may visit this link to gain deeper insights on developing your business and making it a happy place for your employees as well as customers. I have also shared my personal life experiences which might help you navigate through the uncertainties you are currently going through in your entrepreneurial journey.

This is how I did it; if I can, so can you!

JOHN CHERIAN, CO-AUTHOR

A veteran in business strategy and corporate leadership, **John Cherian** has spent years driving organizational growth, fostering global partnerships, and optimizing business operations. His expertise spans strategic planning, market expansion, and enterprise transformation. Through his work, John distills complex business challenges into actionable insights, offering readers a roadmap to navigating modern business dynamics with confidence and foresight.

3

THE LIFE, LEADERSHIP AND LEGACY OF PHILIP SAMUEL

"It's fine to celebrate success but it is more important to heed the lessons of failure."

- Bill Gates

Embracing Change and Defying Odds

Behind every trailblazer is a story of transformation—a journey defined not only by triumphs and successes but also by challenges, calculated risks, and steadfast perseverance. Philip Samuel's life, characterized by unconventional beginnings and hard-fought victories, epitomizes the essence of true leadership.

As the founder of IndFrag Biosciences Ltd., a pioneering company specializing in extracting natural plant ingredients, Philip transformed vision and instinct into a lasting business legacy. His journey underscores that leadership is not merely a product of textbook knowledge but a testament to resilience and resolve in the face of adversity.

For many, entrepreneurship is a meticulously planned initiative. For Philip, however, the path was anything but predictable. Unforeseen opportunities and setbacks shaped his rise as a business leader. Yet, what distinguished him was his extraordinary adaptability, his ability to glean lessons from every circumstance, and his relentless drive to seize those pivotal moments, inspiring others with his unwavering determination.

The Reckless Start: A Life Before Focus

Today, at 77 years of age, Philip still gets excited, and enthusiasm oozes from him whenever he discusses new ideas and innovations. However, all was not the same, say, 50-55 years ago. Philip Samuel's early life stood in sharp contrast to the disciplined focus of his peers. By his own admission, his college years were defined more by playing *Teenpatti*—a popular card game—than by attending classes. Chuckling, he candidly describes his younger self as "reckless," drawn to the thrill of camaraderie over academic responsibility. While his classmates diligently prepared for their futures, Philip's choices distanced him from the structured path of academic success.

This carefree attitude came with a price to pay. The consequences. Failing his final year meant missing the coveted campus recruitment opportunities his peers readily secured. As they embarked on professional careers, Philip was left to retake his exams the following semester. The setback was a deeply humbling experience; however, this didn't bog him down. It marked the beginning of a profound period of self-reflection, perseverance, and determination, showcasing his unwavering resilience in the face of adversity.

Despite his academic struggles, Philip excelled in subjects like physics and chemistry, making his challenges with engineering coursework all the more ironic. However, rather than allowing failure to define him, he chose to embrace it as a learning opportunity. This resolve led him to an unpaid apprenticeship at the Government Tool Room in Guindy Industrial Estate. This seemingly modest role, which he initially saw as a setback, would go on to define and mark the beginning of a turning point in his life. It was during this apprenticeship that Philip discovered his passion for engineering and innovation, setting the stage for his future entrepreneurial endeavors.

The Catalyst: Learning by Doing

His time in that tool room turned out to be more valuable than any degree, equipping him with more practical experience than any college could offer.

This room, filled with the hum-drum of machinery and the hands-on mentorship from seasoned workers, gave him the real-world experience he needed. Distractions may have marked his college years, but here, surrounded by the clanging metal and sweltering machines, Philip found his focus. This hands-on experience, more than any academic degree, was the cornerstone of his career, emphasizing the value of practical learning in professional development.

Victor Nesan, the milling machine operator, became one of the first mentors to recognize Philip's potential. Nesan's unshakable belief in Philip's abilities was instrumental in shaping his early career years.

"He used to leave me to do the job, taking his breaks, trusting that I could manage," Philip recalls. This trust—this trial by fire—gave him the confidence to master the tools of the trade. It was a far cry from the lecture halls of his college, but it was here that Philip began honing the instincts that would later go on to guide his business ventures. The influence of mentors like Nesan is a testament to the transformative power of mentorship in one's career. The renewed Philip recognized the profound impact of mentorship on his personal growth and career development, highlighting how mentors' are crucial in shaping one's professional journey.

Life in the tool room was no easy feat for young Philip. His initial unpaid role was a test of his financial and emotional resilience. Yet, he remained undeterred. Each day, he absorbed the lessons, learning the nitty gritty of the machinery and, most importantly, understanding and acknowledging the value of resilience. This period laid the foundation for his future entrepreneurial journey. His resilience in the face of challenges is a source of inspiration for all aspiring professionals, empowering them to face their own challenges with determination and resilience. a testament to the power of determination in shaping one's career. He went on to apply these learnings and tactics in his subsequent roles at Kunal Engineering Pvt. Ltd. and Carborundam Universal at Madras (CUMI).

It wasn't long before Philip realized that every experience he had was a lesson waiting to be learned, something that would guide him in his future. Take, for instance, his current philosophy of approaching challenges with soft yet firm solutions, something he picked up from Deepak Banker, a managing director at Kunal Engineering Pvt. Ltd.

His stint at CUMI involved working for PZ Abraham, the marketing manager, and RV Krishna, the executive assistant to the managing director. Both men left impactful impressions through their career contributions and attitude toward work.

Under PZ Abraham's guidance, Philip honed his letter-writing skills, intending to build connections and directly address challenges rather than beat around the bush. Abraham's mentorship taught Philip the importance of clear and direct communication in professional settings.

RV Krishna was unafraid of delivering critique, effectively barraging Philip with the drive to pursue what he needed without hesitation. These lessons in effective communication and decisive action are attributes he carries to this day. He rarely hesitates to check an opportunity and never wastes a moment on doubts. Philip fondly recalls these lessons and memories as he talks about his years at CUMI.

CUMI also gave Philip his earliest chance to travel to the USA and learn the process behind glass refractory production so that he could set up a factory in India. He was the youngest member of the team, but his proficiency in mechanical engineering was just as vital. As the technical assistance to the Sales team, Philip had to learn on the job, understand the nuances of the new technology, and work with the American project manager, Pete Bellinger, for four power-packed months. This hands-on experience not only expanded his technical knowledge but also instilled in him the importance of adaptability and collaboration in a global context. Philip's adaptability in an international context is a shining example of how this skill can open doors to new opportunities in one's career, encouraging the audience to embrace change and be open-minded in their professional journey.

His journey of learning never stopped. By this point, Philip had honed his skills, growing more competent by the year. When CUMI offered a straightforward career package with everything planned for him, he refused and strove to forge his own path.

Philip found his calling at Tamil Nadu Industrial Development Corp. Ltd. (TIDCO). Despite working there only for a mere two years, Philip became the go-to expert at identifying and connecting lucrative projects with an agreeable foreign collaboration.

His work at TIDCO not only brought significant projects to the company but also established him as a leader in his field. He was supported by a preeminent IAS Officer, KP Geethakrishnan, who not only interviewed him for the job at TIDCO but mentored him wisely. The man later climbed the ranks to become the Finance Union Secretary in Delhi and continued his career as the honest officer he has always been. Being surrounded by such pioneering mentors propelled Philip's passions and careers, and he recognized this ardently.

Facing the Odds: The Early Risks

After several years of working in venture idea identification combined with project planning and execution roles, Philip was ready for more. But as with many entrepreneurs, his journey was driven by a vague plan. Instead, it was propelled by a sense of adventure and a series of risks that would ultimately pay off. These risks included financial constraints, lack of resources, and the absence of modern communication tools like email or the Internet.

In the early 1980s, when he was at Mettur Beardsell, a manager named Murali approached Philip with a proposition: to get his guidance and start a business. Philip was invigorated by these discussions and agreed. He dedicated his time and effort to researching small foreign companies that could work in traction with local industries. His unwavering dedication and effort in this research phase were truly inspiring, setting a high standard for aspiring entrepreneurs.

Philip's journey was not without its challenges. In an era devoid of modern communication tools like email or the internet, he had to rely on cold calls to connect with potential clients in the U.S. Using the American Consulate's Yellow Pages, he painstakingly reached out to relevant businesses. Out of ten to fifteen companies contacted, a few responded to him. Philip recognized genuine interest from two: JML Optics and DO Industries, located in Rochester, the capital of optics. His determination and resourcefulness in the face of such challenges set a powerful example for aspiring entrepreneurs.

However, everything was not meant to be smooth. The journey to meet these collaborators was filled with obstacles. With no money for airfare, they turned to their networks for help. Balaji, Murali's cousin and an optics expert himself, eventually came through, pledging his wife's *mangalsutra* to cover the costs of their flight.

This act of generosity and trust from their network was a significant factor in their success. It was a gamble, but one that paid off as Philip and Murali successfully negotiated their first business deal. This deal marked the beginning of General Optics Asia Pvt. Ltd. (GOAL) in 1982, chaired by Murali, and set the stage for their future successes.

Following GOAL's success, Philip established Transprojects Eastern Pvt. Ltd. (TPEL), his first consultancy firm, with Murali as his first client. It was a testament to the men's resilience and determination in the face of ambiguity and adversity, which was truly a hard-won situation for both.

The Formation of IndFrag Biosciences: From Risk to Reward

While TPEL marked Philip Samuel's initial venture into the business world, it was the establishment of IndFrag Biosciences Ltd. that cemented his entrepreneurial legacy.

His success with TPEL, particularly in facilitating connections between local and foreign businesses, sharpened his business development, networking, and risk management skills. The decision to found IndFrag was not merely a leap of faith but a calculated move inspired by a unique opportunity.

TPEL's consultancy specialized in two core areas:

1. **Identifying unique venture ideas in the manufacturing sector:** Conducting technical feasibility and economic viability research, selecting promising ideas, and discarding those with less potential.

2. **Securing foreign collaborations:** Connecting selected ventures with foreign partners for technology, marketing, and financial participation.

TPEL offered comprehensive solutions, including identifying foreign collaborators. Among its notable projects were:

- **Titanium Nitride Coating for Cutting Tools:** This project extended tool lifespans through a partnership with BALZERS (foreign collaborator) of Liechtenstein, a small municipality near Switzerland, a leader in high vacuum technology. Interested clients included Bajaj Auto and Sona Steering.

- **Solar Air Conditioning:** Utilizing high-efficiency, patented flat plate collectors in collaboration with WORLDWIDE SOLAR (foreign collaborator) of Perth, Australia, with the JK Group as the client.

- **Color Anodizing of Aluminum Structures:** Eliminating the traditional use of dyes through collaboration with JASON Anodizing (foreign collaborator) of Australia. This project was undertaken for a wealthy start-up entrepreneur.

- **Coal Beneficiation:** Partnered with Roberts & Schaefer Co. (foreign collaborator) of Chicago, USA, leveraging a simple yet impactful process for clients in the energy sector.

TPEL excelled in persuading small but capable foreign companies to collaborate with Indian firms to establish manufacturing units in India. This process involved meticulous negotiation, persuasion, and showcasing the mutual benefits of such partnerships.

While on the lookout for something more exciting, Philip intuitively identified one promising project that involved extracting fresh flowers to create concentrates for fine perfumery. TPEL engaged multiple European companies for the know-how and buyback agreements and successfully convinced Bertrand Freres (BF), a small company in Grasse, France—the perfume capital of the world. However, the project's cost, Rs. 40 lakhs, was deemed too small for TPEL's clients, who were primarily interested in larger-scale ventures. Philip regretfully informed BF, only to discover that Unilever (UL), the multinational giant, owned BF.

Unilever sought an Indian partner to source essential flower extracts for their perfumery business. They dispatched Andrew Attfield from Quest, Unilever's fragrance and flavor division, to meet Philip.

Over an evening at the Taj Coromandel in Madras, Andrew, after a few glasses of wine, convinced Philip to undertake the project independently. Andrew, a seasoned professional in Unilever's fragrance and flavor division, was able to provide Philip with valuable insights and reassurances. Initially hesitant due to the stark differences between consultancy and entrepreneurship, Philip was reassured by Andrew's promise of support from France for the unit in India. A natural risk-taker, Philip made the spontaneous decision to seize the opportunity.

Thus, in 1987, IndFrag (Indian Fragrances) was born.

The company was strategically established in Hosur, an underdeveloped region, enabling Philip to capitalize on government subsidies for businesses in such areas. Coupled with its focus on flowers and herbal extracts, IndFrag quickly emerged as a pioneer in natural ingredients, highlighting the influence of external factors on entrepreneurial success.

IndFrag faced significant hurdles in funding its operations. Multiple loan applications were rejected, yet Philip's resilience and resourcefulness prevailed. Two close friends, Vellayan of the Murugappa Group and Sumant Kapur, a global investor, stepped in as angel investors, providing the equity capital needed to launch his business. Their support accentuated the critical role of personal networks in entrepreneurship.

Despite this, SBI rejected the loan application. However, Philip's determination and connections once again proved vital. Dr. B.W.X. Ponnaiah, Dean of Tamil Nadu Agricultural University and agro-advisor for SBI, intervened, convincing the bank to approve the loan. This critical support highlights the importance of strategic relationships and mentorship in overcoming obstacles.

Setbacks and Perseverance: The Unilever Crisis

From its inception, IndFrag focused on flowers and herbal extracts, positioning itself as a pioneer in natural extracts. They were on a winning streak. Their extracts were the secret behind the allure of famous perfumes like **Christian Dior's** *"POISON"* and **Hermes'** *"24 Faubourg"*.

However, when UL sold BF to Sanofi, Indfrag's business took a hit. Philip could have taken the legal route and sued UL for breaking the 5-year contract. But Andrew, with his strategic insight, advised against it. Instead, they chose to leverage their relationship with UL to find new customers, a decision that proved to be a game-changer.

Reflections: Leadership Lessons from a Trailblazer

As Philip reflects on his journey, he attributes much of his success to the mentors who guided him and the lessons he learned. One of the most valuable pieces of advice came from Deepak Banker, who taught him that the best solutions are often the simplest. Banker's metaphor of using an aluminum rod to shape steel instead of a hammer is a philosophy that Philip applied to many of his business decisions: approach problems softly, avoid unnecessary force, and find the path of least resistance. This simple yet powerful approach to problem-solving has enlightened Philip and empowered him to make effective decisions in his business ventures.

He is also quite cognizant of his luck, which is vital in business. Philip believes that his success is due to God's grace and the fortune of his lessons. He is grateful for his mentors who have all imparted life-long lessons that have aided him during the many successful years in his ventures. His only son chose to work in the company IndFrag, carrying on his legacy and most of the tasks from Philip, who could look forward to semi-retirement with no worries.

It was also luck that he ran into one of his first memorable mentors, Victor Nesan, five decades after his work in the Government Tool Room. Now a big-shot in the business world, Philip enthusiastically offered Nesan a secure job in IndFrag. He believes it always comes down to luck in the business world, along with hard work, instinct and opportunities are vital.

In retrospect, Philip's life is a testament to the power of the entrepreneurial instinct. While many business leaders rely on meticulous planning, Philip's journey has been about seizing opportunities as they come, guided by his instinct. 'Opportunities keep coming to you, and you make yourself,' he says, emphasizing that adaptability and instinct are as important as any business strategy. His story is a source of encouragement for those who believe in the strength of their intuition and its potential to lead to success.

Imparting Lessons: When the Student Becomes the Master

Philip, a humble leader, has always sought opportunities to give back. He takes mentorship seriously, reaching out to new employees or those needing guidance. He steers clear of micromanagement, believing that true mentorship is about nurturing a person's skills, not just overseeing their work.

He recalls a young employee named Gayathri Rajasekhar, who was tasked with conducting her own research and acquiring the desired result within the budget Philip had allocated to her. She was given five lakhs to increase the capacity of a vacuum apparatus from the 400 liters that it could hold at that time to 700 liters, a full 300 liters increase in capacity. When she sent Philip an interim report, he did not bother with it, expecting her to return with the needed result.

And she delivered!

This incident, where Gayathri succeeded based on her conviction and hands-on experience, reinforced Philip's belief in his principles. Philip had realized from his mentors quite early on in life that the potential of having faith in a subordinate's skills and hands-on experience was unbeatable. This belief has holistically shaped his business philosophy and approach to mentorship.

His son, Fabian Samuel, has learned the business this way, stepping up and earning the mantle of IndFrag's leadership through hard work and dedication to the craft. Philip is immensely proud of his son's unique journey that led him to IndFrag, an echo of his career filled with conscious decisions and active opportunities.

These decisions and opportunities include strategic partnerships, innovative product development, and a focus on sustainability. He continues this legacy of teaching many young and aspiring entrepreneurs and workers.

The Legacy Continues: Building for the Future

Today, IndFrag Biosciences is a thriving company, with its influence stretching across international markets. Yet for Philip, success is not just about reaching the top—it's about staying grounded, learning from every experience, and, most importantly, empowering the next generation of leaders.

His unwavering commitment to his employees, especially in rural regions, has created employment for countless people, proving that businesses can be profitable, sustainable, and socially impactful. His dedication to empowering leaders is not just a business strategy but a source of inspiration for all of us.

As he continues to mentor young entrepreneurs, Philip's advice remains consistent and invaluable: Avoid loans, make necessary investments, and learn from failure. It's this simple yet profound philosophy that has carried him through decades of entrepreneurial success.

From collecting used toiletries from star hotels, recycling and distributing to the underprivileged, championing agriculture, investing in young entrepreneurs in waste management, and taking up tasks for the upliftment of society and its people, Philip's energy and dedication to social causes are truly inspiring.

In many ways, Philip Samuel's journey is not about extraordinary achievements but turning the ordinary into the extraordinary. Through hard work, humility, and an unyielding belief in his instincts, he has built a legacy that will continue to inspire future generations of business leaders.

PHILIP SAMUEL, CO-AUTHOR

Born in 1947, Philip Samuel attended school and graduated with a degree in Mechanical Engineering from reputed institutions in Madras.

He started his journey by spending the first eighteen months of his working life in manufacturing companies, making tools and maintaining precision engineering equipment. These were hardcore shop floor jobs, which gave him a solid foundation.

He then moved on to Carborundum Universal Limited, a Murugappa Group Company and an Indo-American JV. Here, he learnt the art of technical selling, project engineering, and management, including training in the parent company for three months in the USA. He had useful exposure to a large and well-managed American company, which gave him his first global exposure.

After 8 years, he moved on to TIDCO and acquired the art and science of start-up techniques, foreign know-how, regulatory approvals, venture funding, and even served on the Boards of various companies.

He shifted to an Indo-British Company, Mettur Beardsell Limited, to head their new project division. He worked for two years to set up a few diversification projects.

At this time in 1982, he left the comforts of a corporate job. He started Transprojects Eastern Private Limited, a consultancy company for the identification of unique venture ideas for small and medium sectors and tying up foreign collaborations for technology, marketing & finance.

After six years, he jumped into entrepreneurship and started Indfrag Limited, which manufactures flower extracts for fine perfumery in collaboration with a small French unit owned by Unilever. The company continued to grow and diversify into plant extracts for Nutrition, Food, Pharma, and cosmetics. Subsidiaries were started in the USA, Europe, and Singapore to establish a local presence globally. Indfrag also acquired an extraction factory in Vietnam near Hanoi, which was a sick unit, in 2014. It has now turned the corner and is making profits.

Indfrag grew to give its shareholders a capital appreciation of 140 times when it was partially sold to an Indian corporate group. Indfrag sold its Nutraceutical extract business but retained all other applications

4

THE LIFE, LEADERSHIP AND LEGACY OF MAHENDRA PATEL

BRIDGES TO TOMORROW THE LEGACY OF LEADERSHIP AND INTEGRITY

Mahendra Patel's journey exemplifies the spirit of *The Life Leadership and Legacy of the TRAILBLAZERS*.

I am often lost in thought, tracing the winding path that life has carved for me—through its countless twists and turns, its trials and triumphs. What stands out above all else lingers long after the fleeting moments of success or the sting of setbacks is the unbroken thread that has run through it all: a quiet, a steadfast sense of purpose. Like a steady current, this purpose has carried me through stormy seas and calm waters, guiding me with a gentle but unwavering hand. It has shaped the way I lead, the way I engage with others, and the way I strive to leave a mark on the world.

As I try to pen this, I offer you a glimpse into my walk—not just as a businessman but as a soul deeply committed to the notion that we are here to leave the world better than we found it. My life has been a dance of empowering others, creating spaces where people can rise, and ensuring that the businesses I've built ripple into the world, leaving a positive imprint on society. For me, a true legacy is not found in the products we create or the profits we accumulate but in the lives, we touch, the values we instill, and the enduring change we inspire.

I understand that the most meaningful success is not measured by wealth or accolades, but by the life, you lead—the hearts you touch, the communities you nurture, and the legacy you leave behind. It is in the quiet moments of giving, in the stories of others' triumphs that echo your influence. In sharing my story, I hope to spark a fire in others—to inspire them to find their purpose, to lead with integrity, and to remember that true success is not in what we take but in what we give.

This is my story—a tale shaped by purpose, guided by the wisdom of mentors, and defined by a legacy I hope will continue to shine long after my time.

The Power of Roots: Learning Leadership from Family and Community

I still remember the day I learned about my grandfather's role as the Mukhi of Ranuj. Much like everything in our family, the story was steeped in tradition, honor, and responsibility. I was just a boy, too young to grasp the weight of the title fully, but the image of my grandfather wearing the Paghadi, the turban gifted to him by the Gaekwad rulers of Baroda, has always stayed with me. It was more than just a piece of cloth—it symbolized leadership, duty, and respect. His position was a beacon of integrity in our small village in rural Gujarat, where simplicity was a way of life and tradition a constant companion.

The stories I grew up hearing, often narrated by my father or older relatives, painted a picture of my grandfather not just as a farmer but as a mediator who represented Ranuj's interests with fairness and authority at the Baroda court. Even though I was just a child, I could feel the respect everyone had for him. He spoke with few words, but people listened when he spoke. His ability to balance justice with compassion became a leadership model I carry with me today.

In our home, there was no need for grand declarations. It was a simple, agrarian life but one rooted in values that transcended wealth or material success. Our family's land, although modest, was fertile, and my father worked tirelessly to ensure that we never lacked. Life in Ranuj was dictated by the seasons—the monsoons, the harvest, and the rhythm of nature itself. I can still picture the joy spreading across the village when the rains filled the lake near our home, flooding the fields with much-needed water and ushering in the promise of a bountiful harvest. These small joys, which most people overlook, shaped my understanding of what truly mattered—community, family, and nature.

But one aspect of our village made me different from the other children. It wasn't the modest house we lived in or the fact that we didn't have electricity—these things were just part of the fabric of life in Ranuj. It was the library. The library was a sanctuary for me, a small, humble building nestled in the heart of the village. My grandfather, who valued education deeply, often spoke about the transformative power of knowledge. It was here, among the dust-covered shelves of the village library, that I first encountered the world of books. I can still recall the feeling of picking up my first book, the smell of the old paper, and the thrill of opening a new door to a world I had never known.

Reading became my escape. It wasn't just about stories or information—it was about expanding my world, about seeing life through the eyes of people from different times and places. I remember how I would lose myself for hours in those pages, fascinated by histories, fables, and philosophies that seemed so far removed from the fields and cows of my village. It was more than a pastime; it was a deep, abiding passion that shaped my life. Even today, as I sit in my office or at home, I often look back at that little library and smile. My love for learning took root there, and it's a love that has never left me. Even now, I make it a point to read two books a week—something I do to honor that early curiosity and keep growing.

But reading wasn't the only lesson I learned from my grandfather. The true lessons came from watching the people around me. My father, in particular, was a constant source of inspiration. As a young man, he had risen through the ranks at Greaves Cotton, a prominent engineering company. I watched him work tirelessly, balancing his career with our family's needs. Even though he had a demanding job, he never once made us feel that we were anything less than his priority. His integrity and dedication to his work were qualities that I admired, and I knew from an early age that hard work was the foundation upon which success was built. But what struck me about my father was how he carried himself with such humility. He didn't flaunt his achievements, but he showed us, through example, that success was not about titles or accolades. It was about doing the right thing, no matter the cost.

My grandfather's role as Mukhi taught me about leadership, responsibility, and the importance of community. My father's career showed me that success could only be achieved through ambition and integrity. The books I read opened my mind to new ideas, philosophies, and ways of thinking that challenged the boundaries of my small world. These lessons formed the foundation of who I am today.

But it wasn't always easy to apply these lessons. I knew that I could never forget the importance of community, that I could never compromise on integrity, and that I had to keep learning if I was to make any meaningful impact. But the path wasn't always clear. There were times when the world felt too large too overwhelming, and I questioned whether I had what it took to navigate it.

I remember my first real job, the first time I ventured into a professional setting. It felt like stepping into a world where everyone played by different rules, and I often wondered if I belonged. But even in those moments of self-doubt, I could hear the voices of my grandfather and father echoing in my mind. "Be fair," my grandfather would say. "Stand by your values," my father would remind me. And it was through those voices that I found the courage to push forward.

The Seeds of Leadership: Early Influences and Lessons

Over the years, as I built my career and established myself in the business world, I never forgot the lessons from my youth. Leadership, to me, was never about power or control. It was about responsibility, empathy, and the willingness to serve others. I saw leadership not as a position to be attained but as a fulfilling duty. As I started my ventures, I carried that sense of duty with me—always striving to lead with integrity and to build businesses that were not just profitable but also impactful.

As a child, I often found myself amid what some might call ordinary games, but to me, these were far from that. Growing up in Mumbai's Aadarsh Nagar, I was surrounded by energy, ambition, and a competitive spirit that seemed to fuel every part of my day. What might have seemed like simple games to others—Gilli Danda, Lagori, and cricket—were the first stages for me to learn the art of leadership. These were the early moments where I first experienced the thrill of bringing people together toward a common goal, the joy of strategizing, and the responsibility of guiding a team through the highs and lows of competition.

I remember captaining the Gilli Danda team in our neighborhood like yesterday. We didn't have fancy equipment or uniforms, just a wooden stick and a few stones, but I took that role seriously. My job was to ensure everyone knew their part, to inspire them when we were losing, and to remind them of the importance of playing fairly. Cheating was never an option for me, even in something as small as a childhood game. It wasn't about the win but about doing things the right way, about honor. That belief would stick with me throughout my life, especially as I entered the professional world. My competitive streak was always tempered with a profound respect for fairness. I knew early on that being a good leader wasn't just about winning; it was about how you won.

My leadership journey didn't stop with games. By reaching secondary school, I found that these early lessons had begun shaping how I interacted with others. I wasn't just focused on my success anymore—I was more interested in helping others succeed. That led to my election as the Speaker of the student parliament in my higher secondary years. I hadn't set out to become the leader of the student body, but when the opportunity arose, I took it with both hands. I was still growing, still learning, but the role required me to be fair, articulate, and decisive—qualities that I realized were fundamental to effective leadership.

I remember standing before my peers, addressing the assembly, with teachers watching from the sidelines. It wasn't just about giving speeches or making decisions but about earning respect. Being the speaker meant that I had to be the voice of my classmates and represent their needs while balancing the rules set by the school. And what struck me most was how those moments of responsibility shaped my character. I was learning to listen, empathize, and make decisions that affected people's lives.

But none of this would have been possible without the foundation laid by my family. My father, especially, was the guiding light throughout my childhood. He taught me by example, showing me what it meant to work hard, persevere, and hold onto your values no matter where life took you. Growing up, I watched him rise through the ranks of Greaves Cotton, a prestigious engineering company, eventually becoming the Director of Sales and Service. What stood out to me the most wasn't just his professional success—the way he carried himself. My father had an incredible work ethic but also a deep sense of humility. He treated everyone with respect, whether they were his colleagues, subordinates, or clients. That respect for others, regardless of their status, became my core principle.

But there was one story that particularly left a mark on me. It was about a decision my father made early in his career that would change his professional life. At a time when he was well-positioned for greater success at Greaves Cotton, he chose to leave the security of his job to take on a challenging new role at Windsor, India. This was not an easy decision. Windsor India was a startup venture focused on setting up a plastics manufacturing plant, and the risks were significant. But my father took the plunge, driven by a belief in the project's vision and the possibility of growth. I saw that decision as a great courage—a willingness to leave the comfort of certainty for the unknown. That kind of risk-taking and forward-thinking would later define my entrepreneurship style.

The sacrifices my father made, the tough choices he had to navigate, and how he balanced his professional life with his family responsibilities taught me invaluable lessons about leadership. More than just the tangible success of his career, the integrity he demonstrated shaped my understanding of what it meant to be a leader. Leadership, I realized, wasn't about claiming authority—it was about serving others, about making decisions that took into account the well-being of the people you were responsible for.

And, of course, there was my grandfather. Though he passed on before I could fully appreciate his influence, I often heard stories about him. My grandfather was the Mukhi of Ranuj, a title with immense responsibility. The Mukhi wasn't just a figurehead—it was a role that demanded wisdom, fairness, and a deep commitment to the community. My grandfather's role as a mediator and his ability to balance fairness and firmness left a lasting impression on me. He was a man of authority, but his authority was always exercised in service of others. From him, I inherited a sense of pride in community service and an understanding that leadership is as much about responsibility as authority.

Looking back, I realize that all these influences—my father's work ethic, my grandfather's sense of duty, and the lessons I learned from playing childhood games—shaped my approach to life and leadership. As I transitioned from adolescence to adulthood, I knew I carried a unique blend of values, experiences, and leadership traits. These early years laid the groundwork for who I would become. They gave me the tools I would need to navigate the challenges ahead, the foundation upon which I would build my career and my ventures.

I felt prepared when I was ready to step out into the world beyond home. I strongly understood who I was and what I stood for. I knew that my future wouldn't be without its challenges. Still, I also learned that the values instilled in me by my family—fairness, integrity, responsibility—would guide me through anything life threw my way. Little did I know that these formative experiences would serve as the compass to help me navigate the obstacles and opportunities I would face in the coming years.

Breaking the Mold: An Apprenticeship in England

At the age of 16, I felt an overwhelming desire to leave my homeland, step beyond Gujarat's borders, and experience the world in a way that went far beyond what I had known. Growing up in rural India, the stories I heard from my elders about resilience, integrity, and the importance of pushing one's boundaries fueled my ambition. Venturing abroad to pursue an apprenticeship in England wasn't just a career move for me—it was a chance to prove to myself and my family that I could navigate the world on my own, break free from the familiar, and pursue something far greater than I had ever imagined.

My first step was when I joined Windsor India, a joint venture my father had helped establish. I saw this as my first real step into the world of engineering. By working there, I could gain hands-on experience, learning the ins and outs of manufacturing and the technical skills essential for any engineer. Windsor, India, was a place where high standards and expectations were the norm, and I threw myself into my work with a passion that impressed my mentors and colleagues. During this time, I gained the technical knowledge and confidence to set the stage for the next chapter of my life: England.

But getting to England wasn't going to be easy. British immigration laws at the time required minors to have a legal guardian in the country, a requirement that nearly stood in my way. That's when Peter Windsor, the owner of Windsor UK, stepped in. Having been a frequent visitor to India, Peter had developed a fondness for my family. When he learned about my aspirations, he took an extraordinary step—he agreed to act as my legal guardian in England. This was no small gesture. Peter wasn't just offering me an opportunity; he was responsible for ensuring my well-being and safety while I was abroad, a commitment that created a bond between us that would last far beyond my apprenticeship.

In August 1965, with my bags packed and a head full of dreams, I boarded a cargo passenger ship bound for England, which was nothing short of an adventure. A 21-day trip across the seas felt both thrilling and daunting. I remember every detail—the various ports we stopped at, the anticipation that grew with each passing day, and the moments of uncertainty as we crossed the rough waters of the North Atlantic. Seasickness was inevitable, and I wasn't immune. But amidst the discomfort, I found camaraderie with the other passengers, many of whom were also far from home for the first time. Together, we shared stories, meals, and laughter, making the most of our days at sea.

When we finally docked in Liverpool, I was a mixture of emotions. Relief, excitement, and exhaustion all came at once. I had only three British pounds in my pocket, the maximum amount permitted by Indian regulations at the time. Yet, even with the thrill of being in a new country, the reality of being alone, far from my family, and in an unfamiliar land began to sink in. But I was determined. I had a purpose, and I wouldn't let anything stand in my way.

Peter Windsor's nephew greeted me at the docks and took me to Kingston-upon-Thames, where I would live with a local family, the Ambroses. Mrs. Ambrose, my host, was kind but strict, teaching me everything from English etiquette to the more subtle social norms. The differences in culture were striking, especially when it came to food. Back home, I was used to a simple, vegetarian diet, but now I found myself facing boiled vegetables, pork, ham, and meats I had never seen before. At first, it felt like an insurmountable challenge. But I was there to learn, to grow, and so, bit by bit, I began to adapt, even trying meat dishes at the encouragement of my fellow boarders.

Adapting wasn't just about food but every aspect of life. From understanding table manners to adjusting to the British way of life, I learned quickly that every day brought something new. At the same time, I was working tirelessly to improve myself in the technical world of engineering. My apprenticeship at Windsor UK meant long days on the factory floor, from 8 a.m. to 5 p.m. I worked with machinery, learned assembly processes, and began understanding the manufacturing world's inner workings. It was hands-on training that was both intense and rewarding.

But my days didn't end at the factory. After dinner, I would attend evening classes from 6:30 p.m. to 10:30 p.m. The pace was grueling, but I knew it was necessary. I was there to make the most of every opportunity, so I pushed myself to excel in my practical work and formal studies. The schedule taught me discipline, time management, and the resilience to continue despite exhaustion. I was learning the technical aspects of engineering and how to balance my personal growth with my professional ambitions.

One of the most important lessons I learned during this time was the importance of communication. Although I was familiar with English from my reading, speaking it fluently in a professional setting was a different challenge. I worked hard to refine my conversational skills, adapting to the British accent and colloquialisms, and over time, my confidence grew. This skill would later prove invaluable as I began working in international business, where effective communication is key to building relationships and trust.

Living on a modest stipend, I learned the value of financial discipline. Every penny counted as I budgeted for rent, food, and transportation. Despite my limited means, I sent money back home to support my family. This was an important step toward independence, and I took pride in being able to support them while learning and growing in my new environment.

The seven years I spent in England were transformative. I entered as a young, eager apprentice, but by the time I left, I had earned a Master's in Industrial Engineering from Cranfield

University. More than just an academic achievement, this degree represented the culmination of years of hard work, resilience, and a commitment to personal and professional growth. I gained technical expertise and developed a broader perspective on leadership, cross-cultural relationships, and the importance of global thinking.

When I returned to India in 1974, I wasn't the same person who had left years earlier. I was a man of experience, ready to take on whatever challenges lay ahead. England had shaped me in ways I could never have anticipated. It tested my resolve, sharpened my skills, and broadened my worldview. As I stepped back into the world I once knew, I did so with the spirit of a trailblazer—ready to embrace new opportunities and continue making a difference.

Looking back, I can see that my time in England wasn't just about gaining an education—it was a rite of passage. It was a journey that tested my limits, expanded my horizons, and set the course for everything that followed. It was the beginning of my transformation from a young man with dreams into someone ready to lead, innovate, and impact the world.

Building Patel Filters: A Vision Realized

When I look back at the pivotal moments in my life, the decision I made at 16 to leave home and venture to England stands out as one of the most defining. At that time, I was filled with excitement and fear—emotions that only a young man, eager to experience the world yet unsure of what awaited him, could understand. My family had always emphasized the importance of education and hard work, but this was different. This wasn't just about going to school or learning a trade—it was about stepping outside the comfort of everything I had ever known.

I was born and raised in rural Gujarat, a village where the pace of life was slow, and the world seemed far away. My father, though, had always encouraged me to think beyond our small circle and dream bigger. He had made sacrifices to ensure we, his children, had access to opportunities he never had. From humble beginnings to a senior role at Greaves Cotton and later in a key position with Windsor India I learned that perseverance and hard work could break any barrier. I was determined to prove to myself and my family that I could do the same.

At Windsor, India, I was able to learn about manufacturing, but my ambition called me to something bigger. The apprenticeship in England wasn't just an opportunity but a challenge that I could not ignore. I wanted to push myself beyond what I knew, test my skills, and see if I could truly make something of myself in a foreign land. It was an unusual step for a boy from my background, but I was ready. I felt like I was meant for more; this was my chance to prove it.

The process of leaving India for England wasn't easy. Immigration laws at the time were strict, especially for minors. I needed a legal guardian in the UK who could take responsibility for me. Peter Windsor, the man behind Windsor UK and a close friend of our family, became my guardian. His belief in me was not just a gesture of kindness—it was a massive responsibility that he took on, and I will never forget the trust he placed in me.

In August 1965, I remember standing at the docks in Mumbai, the city's hustle around me, the salty air mingling with my nervous excitement. As I boarded the cargo passenger ship, I had no idea what awaited me in England. I had read about the country in books and heard stories from others, but this was my first time leaving the familiar. I was nervous, yes, but I was also filled with anticipation.

The 21-day journey was unlike anything I had ever experienced. The ship made several stops along the way—Karachi, the Suez Canal, Malta, Gibraltar—each new place sparking a sense of wonder in me. I was far from home, traveling across the seas to a completely unknown land, yet there was something exhilarating about it.

But the excitement was tempered by the reality of the rough seas. The North Atlantic was a force to be reckoned with, and I wasn't immune to the waves that tossed the ship around. There were days when I felt seasick and homesick all at once. Still, as I looked around at the other passengers, many of whom were also traveling far from their families, I found a camaraderie in our shared experiences. We laughed together, told stories, and tried to make the best of our days at sea.

Arriving in Liverpool was a bittersweet moment. I was filled with excitement, yes, but also with the heavy weight of responsibility. I had just three pounds to my name, and the world ahead of me felt like both an opportunity and a daunting challenge. It was a far cry from the comfort of my home in Gujarat, and I realized I was completely alone in a foreign land.

Peter Windsor's nephew greeted me at the dock and took me to Kingston-upon-Thames, where I would stay with the Ambrose family. Mrs. Ambrose was kind but strict—she was the perfect hostess, ensuring I adapted to British customs. My first few weeks were an adjustment, to say the least. The food was a world away from the vegetarian meals I was used to back home. I remember sitting at the dinner table for the first time, staring at the pork and ham in front of me. It felt strange, almost unnatural, but I began to embrace the differences as the days passed. After all, I was here to learn, and every experience was a chance to grow.

The real challenge, though, was the pace of life. The apprenticeship was demanding. My days were spent working on the factory floor at Windsor, learning the intricacies of engineering and manufacturing. I spent hours each day knowing how machines worked, understanding production processes, and honing my technical skills. But my learning didn't stop there. After a long day of work, I would attend classes in the evening, from 6:30 p.m. to 10:30 p.m., balancing my studies with the grueling work schedule.

It wasn't easy. There were nights when I felt the exhaustion weighing on me when I questioned if I could keep going. But then I would think of my father—the sacrifices he had made to get me to this point—and I knew I had to persevere. The same determination had driven me to take this leap in the first place.

One of the biggest hurdles I faced in England was the language barrier. Though I had learned English from a young age, conversational English was another story. The British dialect, colloquialisms, and accents were initially overwhelming. But as time passed, I started to get the hang of it. I spent my lunch breaks talking to colleagues, asking questions, and immersing myself in the language. Slowly but surely, I became more confident in my communication.

My apprenticeship wasn't just about learning technical skills but also about learning how to navigate a new culture and way of life. The social norms in England differed from what I was used to, and I often observed more than participated. But as I learned, I started incorporating the best of both worlds into my life.

Despite the challenges, a sense of accomplishment came with every step. Every day was a small victory. I had left my home, crossed oceans, and lived in a country where everything was different—yet I was making it work.

Seven years passed in England. I learned the technical aspects of engineering and invaluable lessons about resilience, independence, and cultural adaptation. I was a different person when I finally returned to India in 1974. I was no longer the young boy who had left Gujarat; I had grown into someone who understood the value of hard work and experienced firsthand what it meant to persevere in adversity.

But returning home was not just about what I had learned academically; it was about taking everything I had experienced and applying it to the world I was now a part of. I had seen how businesses in the UK operated, how industries were run, and how innovation was embraced. I knew India needed that same forward-thinking mentality and was determined to bring it here.

My time in England had prepared me for what was to come next: a chance to build something of my own, a business that would not only reflect my technical expertise but also a manifestation of the values I had learned throughout my life. I was ready to take on the world—one challenge at a time.

My Journey with Patel Filters: Building Something That Endures

When I look back at the early days of Patel Filters, I see more than just the birth of a company—the culmination of years of hard work, sacrifices, and lessons learned from failure and success. But the road wasn't always smooth. Building Patel Filters into a successful enterprise was just the beginning of a much larger journey—one that would test my resilience, adaptability, and ability to navigate through a maze of challenges that sometimes seemed insurmountable.

In the late 1970s and early 1980s, India's economy was a volatile place to do business. The country was still under the grip of the License Raj, a system where the government closely monitored every move in business, from sourcing materials to expanding operations. Strict regulations, long delays in acquiring licenses, and unpredictable market conditions created an environment of uncertainty. This was not a time for the faint-hearted. But I had a vision—one that went beyond the immediate obstacles. I believed in India's potential, in its people's ingenuity and resilience, and in my ability to lead Patel Filters through this chaotic landscape.

One of the most pressing challenges we faced early on was securing a stable supply of raw materials. India's economy at the time was highly controlled. The government imposed strict import restrictions, which meant that essential materials for manufacturing were often scarce or subject to long delays. For a growing company like ours, relying solely on imported materials would be a major bottleneck. I knew that without a steady supply chain, we couldn't scale. It wasn't just about having the right materials but ensuring that our operations ran smoothly without interruptions.

This was the first true test of my entrepreneurial spirit. I could have easily blamed external factors—the government regulations, the market conditions, the scarcity of resources—but I chose not to. I decided to take matters into my own hands. I began researching alternative suppliers within India, sourcing locally where possible. But it wasn't enough to just find new suppliers. I needed to ensure that the materials we sourced were of the same high quality as the imported ones. This led me to invest in research and development, exploring ways to improve material utilization, reduce waste, and streamline production processes.

I knew that innovation would be the key to our survival. By the late 1970s, Patel Filters was no longer just a company manufacturing filtration products—it had become a hub for creative problem-solving. I was able to reduce our reliance on imports, improve efficiency, and increase our profitability. But more than that, we became a company known for its ability to think outside the box. We weren't just following the market; we were shaping it.

But navigating the regulatory environment wasn't just about sourcing materials. It was a constant challenge. Every day brought new complexities—import permits, tax filings, government audits—and we were forever battling the system. In hindsight, I realized that the License Raj was a blessing in disguise. While restrictive, it forced us to be more resourceful, disciplined, and strategic. It pushed me to think in ways I never had before.

Rather than viewing regulations as roadblocks, I saw them as challenges that required creative solutions. This was a mindset that I cultivated in myself and the people around me. I forged strong relationships with local authorities and government officials, ensuring that Patel Filters remained compliant. But I didn't stop there. I actively sought out industry network groups that could offer insights and connections to help us navigate the bureaucratic landscape more efficiently. This network became invaluable as Patel Filters grew. It wasn't just about what you knew—it was about who you knew and how you worked with them.

There were times when the weight of the regulations felt overwhelming. I often found myself at my desk late at night, reviewing paperwork, coordinating with government departments, and figuring out how to keep everything moving forward. But I refused to let these challenges define us. I told myself that every obstacle was an opportunity to learn, adapt, and find a better way of doing things.

Market fluctuations presented yet another hurdle. The filtration industry, like many others, was heavily tied to the fortunes of sectors such as mining, chemicals, and paper. These industries were known for their cyclical nature, with periods of high demand followed by sharp downturns. It was a precarious situation that could have easily sunk Patel Filters if we didn't diversify. But how could I expand in an unpredictable market?

I knew that Patel Filters couldn't rely on just one industry to weather market downturns. We needed to diversify our customer base, expand our reach, and introduce new product lines catering to different industrial needs. I looked at the flourishing industries and those growing despite the economic challenges, and I ensured that Patel Filters could serve their needs.

This wasn't easy. Every new market segment required research, adjustment to our manufacturing processes, and often, the development of entirely new products. But with each new line we introduced, we became more resilient. We weren't just surviving anymore; we were thriving. We had clients across multiple industries—mining, paper, cement, chemicals—and we became known for our versatility and reliability.

There were moments when the market seemed unforgiving, when orders dried up, and it felt like we were treading water. But instead of panicking, I reminded myself and my team that this was a phase. Like all cycles, this, too, would pass. And when it did, Patel Filters would be stronger for it.

Perhaps our greatest asset during those turbulent years was our commitment to quality and customer satisfaction. The core of Patel Filters wasn't just its products but the relationships we built. From day one, I had made it clear to my team that we were not just in the business of making filters. We were in the company of making promises—and keeping them.

In an environment where customer service was often secondary to price or speed, Patel Filters stood out for its unwavering focus on client satisfaction. I remember countless instances when clients would request additional modifications to a product or ask for support beyond what was specified in the contract. Most companies would have turned them away, citing extra costs. But I refused to take that approach. Our clients weren't just customers—they were partners. And partners look out for each other.

There were times when we absorbed extra costs to ensure that a client's needs were met, and we worked late into the night to meet a deadline or make last-minute adjustments to a product. But those efforts paid off. Our clients recognized that Patel Filters wasn't just another supplier—it was a trusted partner they could rely on no matter what. And that trust translated into long-term contracts, which became a cornerstone of our stability during uncertain economic times.

Internally, my goal was always to build a company culture that valued accountability and innovation. It wasn't enough for me to simply lead from the top—I needed to inspire my team to think creatively, take ownership of their roles, and embrace challenges as growth opportunities. Every problem, every bottleneck, was an opportunity for us to improve.

When production faced delays or inefficiencies, I didn't just look for quick fixes—I involved the entire team. We gathered in the factory, brainstormed solutions, and worked together to streamline our processes. It wasn't always easy—sometimes solutions took weeks, or even months, to implement. But the results were worth it. We became more efficient, cohesive, and innovative as a team.

That culture of accountability extended beyond production. It became part of the fabric of the company. Whether it was in marketing, sales, or customer service, everyone at Patel Filters was empowered to contribute ideas and take initiative. This inclusive approach didn't just boost morale—it led to practical solutions that helped us scale and evolve.

Looking back on those years, I realize that our challenges were not obstacles but stepping stones. Every setback was a lesson in resilience. Every market downturn taught me the importance of diversification and adaptability. Every regulatory challenge pushed me to become more resourceful and creative. And through it all, I remained focused on one thing: building a sustainable, trusted enterprise.

Patel Filters was no longer just a business—it had become a testament to what could be achieved with persistence, creativity, and a commitment to people. It was my vision coming to life, not just of success in the business sense but of building something that would endure and stand the test of time.

And that, I believe, is what truly defines success.

Mentors and Influences: The Power of Guidance

As I look back, I can't help but feel an overwhelming sense of gratitude for the mentors who played such a pivotal role in shaping the leader I became. Their guidance, wisdom, and unwavering support helped me navigate business challenges and understand what it truly meant to lead with integrity, compassion, and a sense of responsibility. Two figures stand out as the guiding lights in my life—Peter Windsor and my father. Both of them taught me invaluable lessons, lessons that went beyond business acumen and taught me the true essence of leadership.

I remember the first time I met Peter Windsor. During my apprenticeship in England, I was far away from home and still trying to find my place in the business world. Peter was a man of stature— graceful, poised, and deeply respected by everyone around him. He wasn't just the owner of Windsor UK. He was a mentor, a guide, and, to me, a model of what a true leader should be. It's no exaggeration to say that Peter's mentorship completely transformed my outlook on business, leadership, and life.

One of the first things I noticed about Peter was his remarkable punctuality. It wasn't just about being on time—it was about respect for others' time and recognizing the importance of every moment. I still remember standing next to him at the office, seeing how people responded to him. There was a calm authority in his presence that demanded respect without uttering a word. He had a way of making you feel important simply by listening and giving you his full attention. It's something I try to carry with me every day. Peter didn't need to raise his voice to be heard; he led through action and respect.

But what struck me the most about Peter was his balance between authority and empathy. He was a man who knew when to assert his opinion and when to step back and listen. This wasn't something I had fully understood until I worked with him. Peter often told me, "A good leader listens more than he speaks," this advice resonated deeply with me. As I took on more responsibility at Patel Filters, I consciously applied this wisdom in every interaction—whether with my team, clients, or business partners.

When I led Patel Filters, I made it a point to listen to my team members' concerns and ideas. I would sit down with employees at all levels and ask them how they felt, what challenges they faced, and what suggestions they had. I didn't just see myself as the person who gave orders; I saw myself as someone who was there to support and guide them, just as Peter had supported me. It wasn't always easy, especially when tensions ran high or when time was tight, but Peter's influence reminded me that leadership isn't about being the loudest voice in the room. It's about fostering an environment where everyone feels valued, heard, and respected.

Another lesson Peter instilled in me was the importance of structure and organization. He ran his business precisely, and everything, from client meetings to internal communications, was done with attention to detail that left no room for mistakes. I took this lesson to heart. Early in my career, I didn't always appreciate the necessity of systems and processes, but working under Peter's mentorship taught me that a solid foundation was the key to achieving long-term success. The small things—how he managed his calendar, how he prepared for meetings, and the clarity in his communication—made him a remarkable leader.

Watching him operate, I learned that business success is built on meticulous planning and consistent execution. Peter believed success didn't just happen by chance; it was earned through careful work, clear communication, and a commitment to doing things correctly. I carried these values when I returned to India and began leading Patel Filters. Every decision I made, from how I managed our finances to how we approached customer relationships, was done with a sense of responsibility and purpose that I'd learned from Peter.

While Peter was an important mentor in my professional life, my father was the cornerstone of my personal and entrepreneurial development. My father's influence on me was profound; much of what I learned about leadership, integrity, and resilience came from him. He was a man of great vision, having risen from humble beginnings to become a respected figure in the Indian industry. His journey wasn't easy, but it was a testament to the power of hard work, dedication, and an unyielding belief in doing the right thing.

Growing up, I watched my father navigate the ups and downs of business with a quiet determination that left an indelible mark on me. He had a remarkable ability to remain calm in the face of adversity, to make decisions with conviction, and to put the needs of others before his own. I remember countless evenings with him, listening to his stories about his challenges when establishing Windsor, India. He had left a stable job to strike out on his own, taking a huge risk with no guarantees of success. Yet, in his mind, that risk was worth it.

He often told me, "Success is meaningless if it doesn't create value for others." This simple but powerful philosophy became the foundation of my business ethics. My father taught me that profits or accolades don't measure true success; instead, it is measured by your positive impact on the people around you. He believed that a business should serve a greater purpose that went beyond financial gain and benefited society as a whole.

That lesson shaped the way I approached Patel Filters. From day one, I was determined to build a company that wasn't just about making money—it was about creating something that would stand the test of time and contribute to the industrial growth of India. I wanted Patel Filters to be a business that provided high-quality products and positively impacted the lives of its employees, clients, and the communities we served.

What I learned most from my father was the importance of sacrifice. In his pursuit of building something meaningful, he made many personal sacrifices, often putting the needs of his business and employees above his own. Watching him, I realized that leadership wasn't about taking the easy road; it was about making tough decisions to build something greater than yourself, sometimes at great personal cost. I carried this with me as I steered Patel Filters through its challenges. There were times when I had to make difficult choices—whether it was cutting costs during tough economic periods or investing in new technology at the risk of financial strain—but I never lost sight of the bigger picture. Just as my father had done, I was committed to making Patel Filters a company that created value for others.

The combined lessons I received from Peter Windsor and my father formed the bedrock of my leadership philosophy. They taught me that leadership is not about wielding power—it's about building relationships based on trust, respect, and integrity. It's about listening more than you speak, making tough decisions for the right reasons, and leading by example. These values became ingrained in me as I led Patel Filters through its growth and challenges.

Reflecting on those formative years, I realize how these mentors shaped my leadership identity. Peter's structured, detail-oriented approach taught me the importance of clarity and communication. In contrast, my father's resilience and commitment to creating value for others grounded me in a sense of purpose. Their influence continues to guide me to this day, and I carry their lessons with me in everything I do.

In many ways, the success of Patel Filters was not just a reflection of my efforts—it was a testament to the lessons I had learned from two incredible mentors.

Creating a Lasting Legacy: Leadership, Impact, and Mentorship

As Patel Filters evolved into a leading name in the filtration industry, I understood that true success isn't about how much you achieve for yourself but about your impact on others, the lessons you leave behind, and the values you instill in those around you. Building a lasting legacy became my primary focus in business, leadership, mentorship, and social responsibility.

From the beginning, I knew the key to any successful business lies in the people who form its backbone. Leadership, for me, wasn't simply about making decisions or driving profits—it was about nurturing the potential in others and guiding them toward their success. Mentorship became central to my leadership philosophy, shaping how I led the company and the individuals who joined us. It became my mission to give back what I had learned, to help others grow as I had grown, and to ensure that Patel Filters was a place where people could learn, thrive, and feel supported.

Looking back, I realize I was fortunate to have had mentors guiding me when I was just starting out. People like Peter Windsor and my father helped shape who I became as a leader, and it was only fitting that I, too, passed on their wisdom. The impact of mentorship wasn't lost on me. I understood that leadership wasn't just about telling others what to do—it was about helping them find their paths and equipping them with the tools they needed to succeed.

From the start at Patel Filters, I made it a point to mentor my employees, especially those just starting their careers. I remember meeting new team members, getting to know them personally, understanding their strengths and aspirations, and finding ways to support their growth. These weren't just casual conversations but intentional meetings designed to help them grow professionally and personally. I wanted to understand where they were coming from, what they hoped to achieve, and how I could help them navigate the challenges they would inevitably face.

I've always believed that mentorship should be hands-on, not just theoretical. While I shared my experiences and technical expertise with my team, I allowed them to explore and make their own decisions. I wanted them to learn through experience, not just from my advice. For example, when a new project came up, instead of immediately providing a solution, I'd ask my team members to come up with ideas on how to approach it. We'd have brainstorming sessions, and I would offer guidance when necessary, but the ultimate responsibility for the solution was theirs. This was my way of teaching ownership and accountability, two values that I believe are essential in business.

I met regularly with my team, checking their progress and offering feedback. But these meetings were more than just about reviewing performance. They were about creating a space for open dialogue where they could share their ideas, frustrations, and successes. I took the time to listen to them, to hear what they were saying, because I knew that the more I understood them, the better I could support their growth. I knew that investing in my employees' development wasn't just an investment in them—it was an investment in the future of Patel Filters. As the company grew, it became clear that my success as a leader was directly tied to the growth and success of my team. The stronger they were, the stronger the company would be.

But my commitment to mentorship didn't stop with my employees. Over the years, I became increasingly involved in the broader industrial community, sharing my experiences with budding entrepreneurs and young professionals looking to make their mark. I often spoke at industry conferences, sharing the lessons I had learned. But these talks weren't just about recounting my successes—they offered candid lessons in leadership, resilience, and ethical decision-making.

I've always believed that success isn't a zero-sum game. Just because one person succeeds doesn't mean another has to fail. The more I shared with others, the more I realized how much value it brought to me and my audience. I would always get emails or messages from young entrepreneurs looking for advice after my talks. Some were just starting their businesses, while others struggled to keep their companies afloat. It became clear that they didn't just want to hear about my wins—they wanted to know how I navigated the struggles, faced failure, and kept going despite the obstacles.

One of the most rewarding parts of mentoring outside my company was seeing its impact on others. I remember one young entrepreneur who contacted me after one of my talks. He was trying to grow his small manufacturing business but faced financial constraints and stiff competition. We exchanged several emails over the next few months, and I offered him advice on managing cash flow and finding creative solutions to market his product. A year later, he wrote to thank me, saying that my guidance had helped him navigate a tough year and ultimately turn his business around. Stories like this filled me with pride, not because of the recognition but because I had played a small part in someone else's journey toward success.

One core tenet of my leadership philosophy was the belief that businesses should give back to society. Success, I believe, is meaningless if it doesn't create value for others. When Patel Filters began to grow, I was committed to ensuring that our success didn't just translate into profits—it also contributed to the greater good.

We consciously decided to invest in community-focused programs that would have a lasting impact beyond our business.

An initiative I'm most proud of is our work with underprivileged youth. We launched a series of technical training programs, partnering with local schools and community centers to provide hands-on industrial and technical skills training. Our goal was to equip young people with the tools they needed to build successful careers in the industrial sector, opening doors that might have otherwise remained closed to them. Seeing these young people develop into skilled professionals, some of whom later found jobs at Patel Filters, was incredibly rewarding.

We also supported local educational initiatives, sponsoring scholarships for students pursuing degrees in engineering and technology. I believed that by investing in education, we were not just helping individuals—we were helping to shape the industry's future. The more skilled, educated professionals there were, the better the industry would become.

These community initiatives weren't just about giving back— they were part of a larger philosophy that guided everything we did at Patel Filters. We saw ourselves as a part of the community, not separate from it. Our success was built on the support of the people around us, and it was only right that we returned that support in meaningful ways.

I'm not as concerned with the financial achievements or accolades we received over the years. I take the most pride in the lasting impact we made through the people we mentored and the communities we served. The legacy I've built isn't about wealth or personal recognition—it's about creating a business that stands for something greater than itself. It's about ensuring that the values of integrity, trust, and purpose lived on long after I was gone.

I've always believed that a true legacy is not something you can build alone. The people around you shape it, your relationships, and the positive changes you inspire in others. Patel Filters became more than just an industrial powerhouse—it became a place where people found purpose, support, and a shared vision. Employees who started their careers with us went on to achieve remarkable success, and many of them carried forward the values I instilled in them, using those lessons to build their own companies or mentor others in turn.

My greatest satisfaction comes from knowing that I've made a difference in the lives of those I've worked with. I didn't build my legacy for myself—we built it together. It's a legacy of mentorship, trust, and social responsibility, and it's a legacy that will continue to inspire others long after my time.

For me, that's what leadership is all about not building something for yourself but building something that will last, something that will make the world a better place for those who come after you.

Celebrating Life and Legacy

Writing this, I realize how much of my life has been shaped by the people I've met, the lessons I've learned, and the experiences that have molded me. My life is like a beautiful painting by Jackson Pollock; each brush stroke is filled with a color representing moments of triumph and struggle, building and breaking, and always striving for something greater. I've understood that my journey isn't just about the businesses I built, the profits I made, or the recognition I received. It's about the trust I earned, the resilience I cultivated, and, perhaps most importantly, how I've worked to give back to the world around me.

Throughout my career, I've always believed that leadership isn't about standing at the front and directing others—it's about guiding, supporting, and lifting people as they find their way. It's about being there for your team, community, and anyone looking to you for guidance. If there's one thing that stands out to me as I reflect on my life, it's the realization that success, real success, is never an individual accomplishment. It's something collective, something that's built on the shoulders of others, and it's something that's meant to be shared.

I've been fortunate to have several incredible mentors along the way. They've taught me more than just how to run a business or make strategic decisions. They've taught me about life, the importance of integrity, empathy, and doing the right thing—even when it's hard. One of the most valuable lessons I've learned is that true leadership is never about what you can take but what you can give. It's about passing the torch and empowering others to lead, grow, and succeed.

I think about the countless people I've worked with throughout my life—my employees, my mentees, the young entrepreneurs I've had the honor of mentoring—and I feel incredibly proud. I don't just look at them as people who contributed to the success of Patel Filters or any other venture I've participated in. I see them as individuals who carried forward the lessons I've shared, as leaders in their own right who are now creating their legacies. There's no greater sense of fulfillment than knowing that you've helped shape someone else's future and that your guidance has helped them overcome challenges and succeed.

When I first started Patel Filters, it was a simple idea that could solve problems and create value. But as the company grew, I realized that what we were building wasn't just a business but a community. We were creating a space where people could come together, learn from one another, and work toward something greater than themselves. That sense of community, of shared purpose, has been the driving force behind everything we've done, and it's something I hope will continue for generations to come.

But it hasn't just been about the people within Patel Filters. Throughout my career, I've always been deeply committed to giving back to the community. I believe that businesses have a responsibility not just to profit but to make a difference. That's why, alongside our work in the industrial sector, we've always invested in education and skill development, particularly for underprivileged youth. The future of any country, any society, lies in the hands of its young people, and I've always felt it was crucial to provide them with the tools they need to succeed. Whether it was offering scholarships or training programs, I've always believed our success would be hollow if it didn't positively impact those around us.

I remember the first time we launched our training programs for local youth. I was struck by how eager they were to learn, to make something of themselves. Many came from backgrounds where opportunities were scarce, but they had the drive, the hunger for knowledge, and the ambition to create something better for themselves and their families. Watching them grow, acquire new skills, and secure jobs in the industrial sector was one of the most rewarding experiences of my life. That, to me, is what legacy is all about—not just building something that lasts but building something that opens doors for others, changes lives, and creates a ripple effect in the world.

Today's younger generation of entrepreneurs has me hopeful, and I see so much potential. They have the vision, the drive, and the passion to make a real impact, filling me with hope for the future. I believe it's crucial to support and mentor them and share the lessons we've learned. When I speak at conferences or meet with young entrepreneurs, I don't see myself as someone who has "made it" and is now just sharing knowledge from a position of authority. I see myself as a partner in their journey, someone who has been down the road they're walking and is simply offering a hand to help them along the way.

In my mind, leadership is a shared responsibility. It's about creating a space where people can rise to their potential, find their own voice, and lead authentically. It's about knowing that the success of those around you is just as important—if not more important—than your own. This is why mentorship has always been so central to my philosophy. Whether mentoring employees, speaking to young entrepreneurs, or contributing to community development projects, I believe leadership is about lifting others.

Celebrating life isn't just about reaching milestones or accumulating wealth—it's about the relationships you build, the lives you touch, and the difference you make in the world. I've always said that "celebrating life means never giving up, always learning, and sharing prosperity with others." This isn't just a quote; it's a guiding principle I've tried to live by daily. Success is not about the things you accumulate—it's about the impact you have, the legacy you leave, and the positive change you bring to the world.

My story is not just about business or personal success. It's about creating opportunities for others, helping them find their path, and sharing the prosperity from hard work and perseverance. It's about building something that will outlast you and continue to inspire others long after you've gone. It's about making the world a better place for yourself and everyone who comes after you.

I think about the future and see a world full of possibilities. It's a world where leaders can rise, not just in business but in every facet of life. It's a world where integrity, empathy, and social responsibility are valued just as much as profits and productivity. And I hope that, in some small way, my legacy can be a part of that future. I hope the lessons I've learned, the values I've instilled, and the people I've mentored will continue to shape the world positively for future generations.

Being a trailblazer is about more than just breaking new ground—it's about showing others the way. It's about inspiring them to dream big, to lead with purpose, and to make a difference. That's the legacy I hope to leave behind. A legacy of trust, resilience, and generosity. A legacy that continues to guide those who dare to dream, lead, and make a real difference in the world.

And in the end, I know that the true celebration of life is not in the accolades we receive or the wealth we accumulate. It's in the lives we touch, the opportunities we create, and the lasting impact we leave on the world.

MAHENDRA PATEL, CO-AUTHOR

A distinguished leader in the pharmaceutical industry, Mahendra Patel brings decades of experience in sales, marketing, and business development. His strategic vision and deep industry knowledge have played a pivotal role in shaping healthcare solutions and advancing pharmaceutical innovations. As a subject matter expert, Mahendra's insights bridge the gap between industry trends and impactful business strategies, making his work essential reading for professionals navigating the evolving pharmaceutical landscape.

5

THE LIFE, LEADERSHIP AND LEGACY OF ANIL NAIR

REDEFINING SUCCESS

What comes to mind when someone mentions the word "accomplished"? The truth is the meaning varies from person to person. For one, it could mean buying the house they've dreamed of since they were 20. For another, it might be landing their dream CEO role. For someone else, it could simply be the joy of huddling in their living room, surrounded by family.

Regardless of what being "accomplished" looks like, one truth remains: it's a journey built on relentless effort. It's not a status or a fleeting feeling that comes easily—it's earned through countless hours of hard work and dedication.

Anil Nair exemplifies this truth. As the Executive Director of Equitor Value Advisory, a business consulting company; an Independent Director at Kalyan Jewellers India Limited; co-founder of Goodwind Moto Tours; and co-founder and managing partner of

The Pretty Geeky, Anil has ventured into diverse industries, leaving an indelible legacy in each.

Naturally, this brings us to the million-dollar question: how did he do it?

Taking Off to the Summit

The question on everyone's mind when they witness businesspeople and visionaries achieve incredible milestones is always the same: "How did they do it?" It's a question asked in countless magazine profiles, interviews, and red-carpet moments. It's the evergreen curiosity of fans, skeptics, and even critics. The "how"—that tantalizing puzzle—captures us all.

To uncover the "how," let's start where all great stories begin: the beginning.

Anil Nair started like most of us, climbing one rung at a time. From an account executive to an account manager and then rising to the position of Vice President, his journey was a testament to the power of diligence and an unwavering work ethic.

Eventually, Anil became the President of Law & Kenneth (L&K), a pioneering independent Indian advertising agency. When L&K merged with the global powerhouse Saatchi & Saatchi, he was appointed CEO and Managing Partner. For many, such a title marks the pinnacle of their professional climb—a point where one pauses, looks out at the breathtaking view, and asks: "Now what?"

For Anil, the answer was clear: the summit wasn't the end of the journey. It was the beginning of a new challenge.

With over 27 years in advertising and marketing, Nair had built an impressive career. Alongside his professional roles, he nurtured his entrepreneurial spirit, taking on parallel ventures as a semi-entrepreneur. His career spanned both industry-leading agencies and smaller firms, navigating an ever-evolving and dynamic field. The challenges of the industry were stimulating, but beneath it all, Anil felt a quiet dissatisfaction.

He realized that no matter how high he climbed, he was still operating within someone else's framework. The ceilings grew more visible, the boundaries more confining. While working in a multinational company came with perks, Anil couldn't ignore a deeper truth: he was no longer content with his journey being shaped by factors beyond his control. He believed that an individual's true potential was the ultimate driver of success, and he yearned to carve his own path, free from the limitations of traditional corporate structures.

"The Culture Is Not Necessarily What One May Ideally Want It to Be."

To Anil Nair, a team wasn't just a group of people working together—it was a collection of highly motivated individuals united by a shared purpose. However, he observed a critical flaw in the system: when an individual's motivation was crushed, their drive diminished, and they inevitably fell behind. To him, the organizational structures, behaviors, and HR practices of the time were failing to serve individuals effectively. In many ways, they seemed to reward mediocrity rather than excellence.

Nair attempted to challenge these structures, working with those around him to break free from rigid frameworks. However, his efforts didn't yield the results he envisioned. Even as an entrepreneur, he wasn't entirely free to implement his style and vision, as co-founders and collaborators often imposed their own limitations. This lack of autonomy reinforced his belief that his creative potential was being stifled within these confines.

Determined to find a better way, Anil chose to leave the well-trodden corporate path behind and ventured into uncharted territory. He had helped build a company from the ground up and served as its CEO for six years before selling it. Yet, even during this period of accomplishment, he recognized the inherent constraints of operating within a large organization.

After 27 years of navigating the highs and lows of the corporate world, Anil retired from that chapter of his life in 2019. While many might have considered it the end of an illustrious journey, for Anil, it marked a new beginning. Retirement wasn't about slowing down; it was about reigniting his passion for creation. He didn't find fulfillment in merely hitting targets or meeting numbers—what truly excited him was building something from scratch. Having seen firsthand the limitations of corporate life, he knew that satisfaction would never come from working under someone else's vision. His path forward had to be one of innovation and independence.

The Bumps in the Road

A journey isn't truly meaningful unless it tests your mettle. Challenges, obstacles, and roadblocks are the hallmarks of any endeavor worth pursuing. Anil Nair knew this better than most—he understood that the closer you get to your goals, the more intense the challenges become.

His first major roadblock as an entrepreneur came while exploring markets he was passionate about. Among his ventures, building a premium motorcycle touring company stood out as a bold and unconventional move. It was a significant departure from his experience in advertising, but it was also deeply rooted in a lifelong passion he finally had the chance to pursue.

When Nair shared his vision, he faced a wave of skepticism. Many advised him against the idea, warning that India wasn't ready for a premium motorcycle touring company. Some even suggested that the concept would only thrive in markets like the United States or Europe. But Nair trusted his instincts. He believed that India was on the cusp of something transformative—something that aligned perfectly with his passion.

Fueled by Passion, Humbled by Adversity

Anil Nair had always been told that doing what you love ensures that you'll never work a day in your life. The more he reflected on this adage, the more confidence he gained in pursuing his aspirations—dreams fueled by passion and a sense of fun. His journey into entrepreneurship was bolstered by two close motorcycle enthusiast friends who shared his vision and joined him to create the company they had long dreamed about.

But just as their ship was setting sail, it struck an iceberg: the COVID-19 pandemic. As a business rooted in travel and tourism, it was hit hard by the world's abrupt lockdowns. Mere months into pouring significant investments and energy into their dream, borders closed, and people retreated indoors. All plans were halted.

"It was like a three-month-old baby being hit with a hammer," Nair recalls, his voice tinged with the rawness of the experience.

The financial fallout was devastating. Refunds for hotel bookings and other services were nonexistent, and months of uncertainty stretched into what felt like an eternity. The situation looked grimmer with each passing day. Amid this turmoil, the only glimmer of hope came from Nair's education business, which thrived under the circumstances. Remote work and safe shipments allowed the business to keep moving, providing people with accessible products in the safety of their homes.

However, two of the businesses in which Nair had invested the most money fizzled out, leaving behind unsatisfactory results. These moments of failure became profound learning experiences. Through it all, Nair clung to his courage and optimism, believing that something better would eventually emerge from the chaos.

Turning Failures into Insights

Nair didn't view these setbacks as mere failures but rather as valuable lessons to carry forward. He carefully analyzed his oversights, recognizing the importance of choosing the right business models and, equally, the right partners. These reflections shaped his next steps as he exited other ventures, eventually launching a consulting business solo. This marked a significant shift for someone who had initially vowed never to start a business alone.

For Nair, the decision to work solo went against his earlier belief that success was best achieved through collaboration. After spending decades in leadership roles, he had grown weary of the responsibilities that came with running branches, units, or even entire agencies. He found little joy in those aspects of leadership. What he truly desired was to immerse himself in the core of his ventures, actively contributing and staying deeply involved.

This principle guided him through the rest of his entrepreneurial journey. Nair's story is a testament to resilience and the ability to adapt—an enduring reminder that even in the face of crushing adversity, there's always an opportunity to rebuild.

The Process of Looking Back

Once you embark on a new path, whether you realize it at first or not, everything changes. The shift from corporate life to entrepreneurship is a leap that transforms not just your career but also your mindset, priorities, and work ethic. It's a journey that few return from, as the difference is profound and irreversible.

For Anil Nair, the journey was marked by questioning the conventional path. The well-trodden route of studying, earning a degree, working for a set number of years, and retiring never appealed to him. His ambitions lay elsewhere—working not for others but for his own passions.

In contrast to traditional expectations, entrepreneurship often carries the misconception of laziness. In reality, it demands a higher pace and intensity than most corporate roles. Work-life balance becomes almost nonexistent, but there's a unique thrill in setting your own pace. It's like running on a treadmill where you control the speed—and that autonomy fuels a deep sense of purpose.

While others assumed that Nair had retired, become lazy, or simply slowed down because he wasn't constantly flying out for work or buried in endless tasks, he saw things differently. From his perspective, he was busier than ever, operating at a higher level of productivity and creating wealth for himself and others. For him, these years were anything but idle—they were transformative.

The Philosophy of Longevity

Anil Nair's entrepreneurial journey has spanned five years so far, and he has no intention of stopping anytime soon. He doesn't plan to retire at 58, or even at 60. Instead, his goal is to align his career span with his health span, ensuring that the two intersect seamlessly.

This philosophy—of bringing your health span, career span, and lifespan as close together as possible—is one that he frequently shares with others. According to Nair, "Ideally, your health span and lifespan should be the same. The aim is to ensure you don't spend too many years in poor health. If the three lines—life span, health span, and career span—come close to each other, I think that's a life well-lived."

To Nair, the career span isn't just about working; it's about contributing and creating. He views his five years of entrepreneurship not as isolated moments but as a continuation of the lessons he accumulated over 27 years in corporate life. These years were filled with successes and mistakes, the latter being crucial to his growth.

Gratitude for Failure

As he reflects on his journey, Nair acknowledges a colossal mistake early in his entrepreneurial career. While external factors like the COVID-19 pandemic played a significant role, he admits that his own mindset and decisions also needed recalibration. In hindsight, he's grateful for the challenges that COVID brought into his life, as they forced him to confront and reassess his choices.

"Those failures are always necessary," Nair emphasizes. They served as a mirror, showing him that his initial approach to entrepreneurship wasn't conducive to long-term growth. Through those reflections, he discovered new perspectives and strategies, proving once again that even setbacks can be catalysts for success.

For Anil Nair, there's no going back. The path forward is clear—one of continual learning, creating, and building a legacy that aligns with passion, health, and purpose.

Lessons in Mistakes and Clarity

If Anil Nair had never made those mistakes, he might never have learned the critical skills needed to build strong teams, navigate new markets, or identify the right focus areas. Alternatively, these lessons might have come much later in his journey, delaying his growth. Mistakes, while challenging, became gateways to self-discovery and invaluable insights.

As his journey progressed, Nair couldn't help but notice a recurring pattern among other entrepreneurs. In their relentless pursuit of success and a lasting legacy, many seemed to lose their passion along the way. He saw entrepreneurs burning out, breaking down, and ultimately falling apart. This brought a sense of sorrow as he reflected on the sacrifices that led so many to lose the very fire that drove them in the first place. While Nair himself found peace in his journey, he remained deeply empathetic toward those who struggled, recognizing it as an unfortunate fate many entrepreneurs face.

The clarity and focus Nair maintained throughout his own path, he attributes to the people around him. He fostered relationships built on honesty and trust, encouraging those close to him to be brutally honest with him—just as he was with them. This open communication created a foundation of mutual understanding, ensuring there was no room for miscommunication or misunderstandings. It was this transparency that kept him grounded and aligned with his vision.

A Helping Hand Along the Way

Every transformative journey is shaped by the people who guide, inspire, and challenge us. For Anil Nair, these guiding hands came in the form of mentors, colleagues, and thought leaders who profoundly impacted his perspective.

One such figure was his senior partner, Praveen Kenneth. More than just a business partner, Praveen was a guide, a confidant, and a friend who felt like an elder brother. Their partnership and shared experiences left an indelible mark on Nair, shaping his approach to leadership and entrepreneurship.

Beyond personal mentors, Nair also drew inspiration from thought leaders like Anthony Robbins, widely regarded as one of the world's best personal coaches. Attending Robbins' programs proved to be life-changing, helping Nair refine his management skills and reshape his mindset.

Additionally, Nair's passion for reading introduced him to modern philosophers like Naval Ravikant, author of *The Angel Philosopher*. Ravikant, along with Robbins and figures like Anthony Bowden, helped shift Nair's worldview and thought processes. These influences pushed him to examine his life more deeply, engaging in meaningful conversations with colleagues who shared his commitment to self-reflection.

One pivotal moment stands out in Nair's memory—a leadership seminar by Tony Robbins. On stage, Robbins declared, "The decisions you take and don't take shape your destiny." This statement struck a chord with Nair, offering him a moment of sudden clarity. He realized that while people are often consumed by the decisions they make, they tend to ignore the decisions they avoid as if those choices—or the lack thereof—don't hold equal weight in shaping their lives.

This revelation became a cornerstone of Nair's philosophy. The understanding that both action and inaction play critical roles in defining our destiny inspired him to approach life and business with a renewed sense of purpose and intentionality.

A Moment of Awakening

The seminar was a turning point for Anil Nair, forcing him to critically appraise the trajectory of his career. For the first time, he paused to truly evaluate his position, the time he had left, and where he wanted to go. It jolted him out of the haze of comfort that had settled around him, making him question whether the "comfortable" life he had built would truly fulfill his deeper desires.

Nair reflected on the three spans that define a person's life: the health span, the career span, and the lifespan. If the average lifespan is around 80 years and the typical career span lasts only 30 or 40 years, what happens to the remaining decades? For Nair, the thought of spending those years idle or aimless was unacceptable. He decided then and there that even at 58 or 60, it's never too late to rediscover yourself and start anew. And in many ways, that realization marked his true beginning.

The Words We Need Most

Grit, determination, and self-awareness are essential for anyone venturing onto a new or unconventional path. This brings us to a question readers often ask when exploring success stories: "How can I do it?"

For Anil Nair, the answer is clear: to lead a fulfilling life and make the right choices, you must create value for those around you. This principle guides his ventures and relationships, where he demands outcomes that are undeniable—products, services, or ideas that validate their existence through the value they deliver.

Entrepreneurs navigate the world by identifying and filling the gaps in business, making life easier for consumers in ways they might not even realize they needed. When people approach Nair for advice about moving into entrepreneurship or embarking on a new path, he emphasizes one critical aspect: self-awareness.

"Know yourself," he urges. He challenges them to reflect deeply on their values, their sources of joy, their discomforts, and their aspirations. Questions like "Who am I?" and "What am I doing right now?" are, in his view, essential starting points for any transformative journey. These were the very questions he asked himself after that seminar, leading him to carve out a new path.

Redefining Success

Another integral lesson Nair shares is the redefinition of success. In a society that glorifies achievements and vilifies failures, Nair believes success should never be the ultimate goal. Success, he explains, isn't a fixed destination—it evolves with you, changing as you grow and adapt. It's a process of continual learning, improving, and becoming.

This philosophy inspired his book, *License to Fall*, written for those who dream of trying something new but fear the possibility of failure. Nair hopes to shift the narrative, encouraging people to embrace failure as a necessary part of the journey. To him, falling isn't the opposite of success—it's a step toward it.

Lessons from the Fall

In his book *License to Fall*, Anil Nair dedicates nine chapters to a profound idea: shifting the focus away from fearing the fall and instead seeing it as an opportunity to decide what to do afterward. The lessons he shares are not just about resilience but about actively redefining failure as a steppingstone to progress.

One of Nair's central themes is the importance of self-care. He emphasizes that overworking yourself to the point of poor health serves no one. He frequently refers to the concept of the three spans—life, career, and health—and stresses the significance of aligning these spans. The closer they are in length and quality, the more fulfilling your life will be. Work should not run you into the ground, as it often ends the moment your health is permanently compromised.

His final message is simple yet powerful: the importance of trying. Nair's journey into entrepreneurship began with a single moment of clarity at a seminar. From that point on, he knew he could never return to the comfort of his old life. If he had chosen to remain in his steady, predictable position, he might never have reached the heights he enjoys today. Entrepreneurship, he explains, is about taking risks and understanding that every result—whether success or failure—provides a valuable lesson. The fear of failure should never stand in the way of trying.

"Try something new. Even if you fall, it doesn't matter. Continue learning. Be grateful, be kind, and most of all, be human. Take care of yourself." These words, which fuel Nair's philosophy, are what continue to inspire him and those who look to him as a role model.

All Things Considered

When one reflects on Anil Nair's story, the thought arises: "Maybe it really is that simple."

He approaches failure as a universal experience, one that people should embrace rather than fear. He views financial loss as something that can be recovered and sees the risks of business as normal, surmountable challenges. His perspective reframes entrepreneurship and life, breaking them down into manageable human experiences.

Nair also delves into the difference between being rich and being wealthy. To him, wealth isn't about the accumulation of money but about using it to create value—for oneself and for others. He reminds us that in a life filled with endless opportunities, nothing is more important than doing what brings you joy.

Whether it's working with his motorcycle touring group, his consulting firm, or his technology company, Nair finds joy in the small moments—like sitting with young coders, listening to their ideas and learning from them. He remains acutely aware that these moments wouldn't exist if he had chosen to stay within his comfort zone, avoiding challenges and risks.

In the true spirit of a Trailblazer, Anil Nair exemplifies what it means to stand apart: knowing yourself, leaning into your passions, and moving forward with purpose. His journey leaves readers with one profound question:

"How will you build you? Don't waste this life. Try something."

ANIL NAIR, CO-AUTHOR

Before starting his second innings as an entrepreneur, Anil had been a storyteller on behalf of brands for most of his career. He spent 27 years in the marketing & advertising industry at the helm of globally renowned companies like Saatchi & Saatchi in India. He was the Co-founder of one of the biggest independent agencies in India - Law & Kenneth, which was merged with Saatchi & Saatchi in 2014, which Anil went on to lead for years. He played a significant role in helping many MNC brands script their success in India. But his core expertise lies in building powerful local brands from scratch & helping them stand on their own amongst global giants. He has worked on blue chip brands like Coca-Cola, Dettol, Renault, Sony, HSBC, Emirates, Skoda, Thomas Cook, Hero Motocorp, ITC, Pepperfry, Jockey & Kent, etc.

Anil has been ranked 15th most influential person in the advertising and media industry in India by Economic Times, India's leading business daily, in the last decade. Anil is currently in his second innings as an entrepreneur, board advisor, and investor. Apart from Goodwind Moto Tours, he co-founded The Pretty Geeky, a children's edu-games company, an investor in an OTT content creation company, and a specialty E-com portal in the luxury space. He is an independent director on the board of one of the largest jewelry companies in India - Kalyan Jewellers. He is on the board of a global packaging solutions company - Pacfora. Apart from these,

Anil is also a partner and Executive Director of a top-rated business consultancy - Equitor Value Advisory. Anil is also an enthusiastic and experimentative cook, a passionate fan of Arsenal FC, a compulsive traveler, and a self-appointed master of red wine.

6

THE LIFE, LEADERSHIP AND LEGACY OF YADAVALLI SUBRAMANYAM

THE HUMBLE LEADER

Behind every trailblazer is a story of resilience, transformation, and an unwavering commitment to making a difference. Yadavalli Subramanyam's journey is one such tale—a life marked by unrelenting determination, the courage to adapt, and a profound belief in the strength of humility. From modest beginnings as a ward boy to his current role as CEO of Apollo Hospitals, Yadavalli's journey is a demonstration of leadership that grew from challenges and thrived on opportunities. His humility, despite his towering achievements, is a quality that resonates with all.

You may not know this, but in the nascent stages of his career, Yadavalli explored the entrepreneurial world, displaying ingenuity and grit as he navigated uncharted waters. However, it was his transition into the healthcare sector that became the cornerstone of his life's work. Joining Apollo Hospitals—an institution that revolutionized Indian healthcare by stepping into private healthcare at a time when the sector was primarily state-run—he became an integral part of its transformative journey. Over decades, he has been part of Apollo's growth in a rapidly evolving landscape, shaping its presence and impact in India and internationally, ensuring world-class healthcare reaches countless lives.

For Yadavalli, leadership has never been about titles or accolades—but service, empathy, and resilience. His unwavering commitment to service, stemming from his own experiences, has continuously fostered a culture of innovation and compassion, strengthening its mission to deliver exceptional care. By fostering this culture, he has not only advanced Apollo's mission of providing world-class healthcare but also instilled a deeper understanding of the interconnectedness of every role within the organization—from ward boys to CxOs.

Yet, Yadavalli's story extends beyond only professional achievements. It has been a journey of continuous retrospection, introspection, gratitude, and an enduring commitment to uplifting others. By constantly emphasizing mindfulness and reflection, he has inspired not only those within the confines of the hospital walls but also countless others who look to his example. His legacy is a stark reminder that true leadership is measured not by authority or personal power but by the positive impact left in its wake.

Yadavalli Subramanyam's life is a feat of purpose-driven leadership, where humility and service form the foundation for extraordinary success. His leadership only exemplifies that true leadership lies not in seeking power but in empowering others and leaving a lasting impact on the lives touched along the way.

Yadavalli's Journey to Leadership...

Let's start at the very beginning.

Yadavalli's life is a tale of resilience, determination, and transformation—an inspiring narrative that wound its way from the modest lanes of Andhra Pradesh to the pinnacle of leadership at Apollo Hospitals. Hailing from the quaint village of Nandigama in the NTR district, Yadavalli was born into a deeply traditional Telugu Brahmin family rooted in Andhra Pradesh.

While his father worked as a government electrical engineer, his mother was a homemaker. Together, they nurtured a warm, close-knit atmosphere in a large joint family, where 20 to 30 people lived under one roof. Growing up in this environment, rich in traditions and values, gave young Subramanyam the priceless opportunity to learn from his elders and gain life lessons that extended far beyond the pages of any textbook.

Born into a modest, middle-class family, Yadavalli's upbringing had its own challenges. Financial constraints meant he could not attend expensive private or convent schools. In fact, his early education unfolded in the humblest of settings. He studied in a small government school with an infrastructure of only two classrooms. Much of his education took place outdoors, under the shades of trees, amongst nature, which shaped his perspective. While the lack of infrastructure and other resources could have been lamented, young Yadavalli found beauty in the austere circumstances. He embraced the experience, finding joy in learning amidst nature and cherishing the life lessons imparted by his teachers. Studying amidst chirping birds and nibbling squirrels, he absorbed lessons in a way few of today's children could imagine.

The journey, however, wasn't without its share of obstacles. The 10th-grade board exams loomed large as a daunting challenge, and he stumbled, falling short by just one mark in social studies. But fate had other plans. To give you some context, back then, nothing was more important than passing the 10th standard or matriculation—it was considered the ultimate milestone in school education, much like how the 12th board exams are viewed today. Luckily for him, the Andhra Pradesh government at the time introduced moderation marks to address the high failure rate. This policy gave him the lifeline he needed to move forward. With renewed determination, he pursued 'Science' in his intermediate years, driven by a growing passion for the healthcare field.

Yet again, Subramanyam's path to higher education was marked by ingenuity and sacrifice. With his father retiring from the government services, financial constraints tightened their grip. While pursuing his undergraduate degree (B.Sc.), he worked various jobs to support his education and family. One such job involved painting streetlight poles, where he earned money in the mornings to contribute to household expenses and attended college in the afternoons. These formative years were marked by resilience, resourcefulness, and a strong work ethic. Despite having limited resources, his father precedented his education. Somehow, he managed to secure funds for young Yadavalli to attend a coaching center, a significant step toward his goals. He completed his degree against these odds and stepped into the workforce.

As I nudged him to share more about his past, he began to reflect on moments he rarely revisits these days. With the weight of immense responsibilities on his shoulders now, reminiscing is a rare luxury for him. But as he leaned back and chuckled, Yadavalli recounted one of those unforgettable instances—one he described as a moment when he thought he was truly done for. Yet, it was his unshakable ethics and grounded nature that ultimately came to his rescue.

He painted a vivid picture of his days as a pole painter, a phase of his life marked not only by its physical demands but also by the significant personal and professional challenges it brought. One particular incident stood out in his memory—a tragedy that still weighs on him. One of his workers, a young and energetic man, suffered a sudden heart attack on the job and passed away. The tragedy sent shockwaves through his team. The shock of the incident was compounded by a wave of anger and grief from the other workers, who initially directed their blame toward him, holding him accountable for the young man's death.

He admitted that it was one of the most challenging situations he had ever faced till then. Yet, what stood out during that challenging time was the way he had always treated his workers—with respect, compassion, and a genuine sense of responsibility. His unwavering humanity didn't go unnoticed. The family of the deceased worker stepped forward to defend him, making it clear that the young man's passing was a result of natural causes and not negligence on his part.

Listening to him recount this part of his journey felt like uncovering a story within a story, one that not only revealed the hardships he had faced at such a young age but also highlighted the principles that had molded the person he had gone on to become.

He began his career as a ward boy at a small diagnostic center—a role that required him to perform modest tasks such as serving tea and preparing patient beds. Yet, even in this seemingly simple job, he stood out. With dedication and a genuine curiosity to learn, he turned every small responsibility into an opportunity for growth. His eagerness led him to acquire new skills, including operating CT scans. This marked a turning point in his career as he transitioned from being a ward boy to becoming a radiographer. His ability to build strong connections with both doctors and patients further opened doors, eventually leading him into the world of marketing.

Over time, he assumed responsibilities in marketing, leveraging his ability to build relationships with doctors and bring in patients to the diagnostic center. His contributions were recognized, and he eventually became the head of the marketing department. Inspired by his growth and armed with the confidence he gained, Yadavalli ventured into entrepreneurship, which beckoned him next. He established his own diagnostic center, running it successfully for three years.

Despite his business's success, he realized that the demands of entrepreneurship were taking a toll on his time with his family, particularly after the birth of his first daughter. Prioritizing family, he decided to dissolve his business and join Apollo Hospitals as a marketing executive. This decision marked the beginning of an illustrious career with the organization. Dr. Sangita Reddy's mentorship guided him in climbing the corporate ladder.

Over the years, his hunger for learning became the hallmark of his career. Balancing work and study, he pursued and completed management courses at renowned institutions like IIM Ahmedabad, IIM Bangalore, UC Berkeley, Singapore Management University, Kellogg School of Management, and Wharton. These experiences shaped his strategic vision and leadership skills.

Today, Mr. Yadavalli Subramanyam serves as the CEO of Apollo Hospitals International, spearheading the establishment of healthcare facilities both in India and abroad. His journey from a boy studying under trees to a global leader in healthcare is a testament to perseverance, adaptability, and the relentless pursuit of excellence.

Retrospecting...

Yadavalli's unwavering passion for the field has been his driving force. This passion, identified early in life, not only motivated him to pursue a career in healthcare but also to start from the ground up as a ward boy. Acknowledging the role of mentors in shaping his professional and personal growth, he credits four key individuals who significantly influenced his journey.

Yadavalli's father was his first mentor and a constant source of inspiration. It was through him that young Subramanyam instilled the perspective of viewing conflicts as challenges and opportunities. This mindset became a foundation for Yadavalli's approach to life and work, and he rightly attributes much of his success to his father's teachings and influence.

Professionally, Yadavalli holds Dr. Sangita Reddy in the highest regard. He describes her as a teacher and philosopher, a guide who has mentored him at every step of his professional journey, imparting crucial lessons on what should and should not be done. He describes her as his Guru who brought him from darkness to light; in Sanskrit, Guru means a preceptor who shows others knowledge or light and destroys ignorance or darkness ('Gu'= darkness or Agyana and 'Ru'= who brings you to light or Gyana). One of her key teachings that has stayed with Yadavalli to date was the importance of identifying what is wrong as the first step toward defining what is right. He openly credits her mentorship as a cornerstone of his achievements in his personal and professional life.

Not sidelining the sacrifices on the home front, Yadavalli also highlighted his wife's unwavering support as a crucial factor in his success. The demands of a healthcare career, which operates 24/7, leave little room for conventional work-life balance. He is deeply grateful for his wife's understanding, support, and timely advice, which have continuously enabled him to navigate the challenges of his profession and pursue his ambitions.

Beyond these three figures, the fourth, which is the most important Yadavalli, accentuated his mother's unparalleled influence. While he refrains from categorizing her as merely an inspiration, he considers her the essence of his existence—his breath, the very reason for his being. Her influence is profound and deeply rooted in his personal and professional life.

Commitment to the Journey despite Hurdles

Reflecting on his remarkable journey with Apollo Hospitals, he spoke with a quiet intensity that left no room for doubt about his dedication. For him, commitment isn't about a single defining moment. It's something that is reaffirmed with every passing minute, every second.

Yadavalli drew a striking parallel between healthcare and the military, underscoring the relentless, round-the-clock nature of the field. He stressed that healthcare isn't just a job; it's a calling that demands a deep level of responsibility. Unlike fields rooted in entertainment or leisure, healthcare requires a commitment that comes from within, a commitment that must be lived and breathed every moment.

What struck me most was how he vividly painted the emotional landscape of healthcare—a place where life and death constantly collide. "On the same floor," he said, "you might find one room mourning the loss of a loved one, while just down the hall, another family is celebrating the birth of a child. This stark contrast is not unusual; it's part of the rhythm of life in healthcare."

It is clear that these extremes have profoundly shaped him. Yadavalli admitted that navigating the highs and lows of human emotion—the elation of a newborn's first cry and the sorrow of a final goodbye—leaves a lasting imprint. "To truly thrive in this field," he said, "you have to embrace these realities. You need to find meaning in them, inspiration even, because without that constant sense of purpose, the weight of it all can feel overwhelming."

For Yadavalli, this ability to find inspiration amid the challenges of healthcare is what keeps him steadfast in his commitment. It's not the accolades or recognition that drive him, but the understanding that his work touches lives in ways that few other professions can.

As he spoke, I couldn't help but feel that his dedication wasn't just a decision he had made years ago—it was a choice he continues to make, moment by moment, with every heartbeat of his journey.

Allies, Adversaries, and Overcoming Challenges: Yadavalli's Philosophy

As our conversation shifted toward the obstacles he's faced, Yadavalli's perspective was both thought-provoking and inspiring. He firmly believes that challenges and adversaries are not only inevitable but essential for personal and professional growth. Comparing life's struggles to the natural balance of day and night, he explained, "If you don't have night, you don't have day." To him, obstacles aren't just disruptions—they're catalysts that push individuals to innovate, strengthen their resolve, and make meaningful contributions.

He noted that, throughout his career, the people who challenged him far outnumbered those who actively supported him. Yet, he holds no bitterness; in fact, he considers those challengers to be some of his greatest mentors. "When people challenge you every day," he said, "you grow more powerful, innovative, and capable of contributing better." He viewed their resistance not as an impediment but as an opportunity to refine his skills and ideas.

When asked to share an instance, Yadavalli described the intricate process of introducing new systems in healthcare—an environment where change is often met with resistance. Even when a new process is designed with the best intentions, there will always be people who push back, sometimes suggesting alternatives that are unlikely to work. However, instead of seeing these individuals as adversaries to be defeated, Yadavalli adopted a different approach. "You must treat the concept they propose—not the people themselves—as the problem to address," he explained. "By innovating and presenting a better system, you can gain their support."

For Yadavalli, moments of resistance were not obstacles but invaluable lessons in leadership. The opposition he faced inspired him to dig deeper, refine his ideas, and find solutions that balanced innovation with practicality. He emphasized that these challenges were instrumental in shaping him into a more impactful leader, capable of navigating complexities and driving meaningful change.

Yadavalli's perspective on success is clear: it's not about avoiding challenges but about embracing them. He sees resistance as an opportunity—a chance to learn, grow, and transform opposition into collaboration. As he shared these insights, it became evident that his journey is a testament to resilience and the power of turning adversaries into allies on the path to progress.

A Journey Forged Through Challenges

As must be quite evident by now, challenges, Yadavalli believes, are a constant, both in the past and present. Yet, he perceives these challenges as opportunities for growth, which have continuously shaped his journey and provided valuable lessons along the way.

One of his earliest challenges as a child, he recalled, stemmed from transitioning from a Telugu-medium school to studying intermediate and degree courses in English. He vividly remembers the first day when he couldn't understand a word his teacher was saying, and how he felt lost and out of place. Adjusting to the language barrier was a significant hurdle, as he initially struggled to understand his coursework. Despite these tribulations, he persevered and adapted to the new medium of instruction. This, however, was just the tip of the iceberg.

Challenges do not stop to take a breath for anyone. And neither did they for Yadavalli. Especially in healthcare, challenges are ever-present.

The COVID-19 pandemic was a particularly testing period for Yadavalli and his team. The fear of the virus led to a shortage of healthcare workers, as nurses were withdrawn by their families, and doctors were in limited supply. Despite these challenges, patient load surged to four to five times the usual capacity. It was a time of immense pressure but also one of innovation and problem-solving.

Reflecting on those experiences, Yadavalli reiterated that challenges are not conflicts but opportunities to learn, innovate, and grow. Each challenge, whether personal or professional, has been a stepping stone, enabling him to take the next step in his journey. This transformation from obstacles to opportunity is a powerful reminder that challenges can be the catalyst for personal and professional growth.

When asked if he ever hesitated or had second thoughts about taking on any of these challenges, Yadavalli shared a perspective grounded in personal choice. According to him, life presents two paths: one can either embrace challenges as opportunities to grow or avoid them, perceiving everything as a risk. He believes the biggest risk in life is avoiding risks altogether. This emphasis on personal choice empowers us to take control of our lives and face challenges head-on.

Illustrating this point, he compared his outlook to that of a soldier stationed in rugged terrains. What drives the soldier who lives through harsh climatic conditions like freezing temperatures to be constantly vigilant and aware of the ever-present threat of a bullet? The soldier's motivation to remain steadfast in such conditions stems from an internal drive, not external factors. This is the importance of self-inspiration. While external sources of motivation can be helpful, true resilience and determination come only from within. This emphasis on self-inspiration reinforces the idea that we all have the strength within us to overcome challenges.

For him, taking ownership and facing challenges, even in scenarios as demanding as managing the COVID-19 pandemic, is a matter of choice and self-motivation. It is this internal inspiration that enables one to face obstacles with courage and move ahead in life.

Yadavalli has faced numerous challenges throughout his career. Still, two stand out as pivotal moments that tested his resilience and resolve: the early days of Apollo Hospitals and the COVID-19 pandemic.

The first significant challenge came during the establishment of Apollo Hospitals in India. At the time, the idea of private healthcare was virtually unheard of—healthcare was considered the sole responsibility of the state. Convincing people, medical professionals, and institutions that private corporate hospitals could deliver better services through collaborative models was no small feat. There was resistance from all over—the society, doctors, nursing homes, and government hospitals alike. "It wasn't an easy thing. It was the greatest challenge we had to face," he recalled. Yet, through sheer persistence and hard work, Apollo didn't just overcome these hurdles—it laid the foundation for what is now India's private healthcare industry. Today, private hospitals in the country offer world-class care, reducing the need for patients to travel abroad for treatment. Yadavalli proudly reflected on this transformation, saying, "What started as a challenge has now become one of the biggest industry in the country."

The second defining challenge was the COVID-19 pandemic, a time Yadavalli described as one of his life's most emotionally and physically draining periods. The pressure on healthcare workers was immense, as they faced daily tragedies and moments of helplessness. "There were times when we felt utterly powerless," he admitted. Patients arrived full of hope, but despite every effort, not every life could be saved. The heartbreak was compounded by the harsh protocols of the time—families were not allowed to see or touch their loved ones before cremation, adding an additional layer of grief to an already devastating situation.

The pandemic wasn't just a professional challenge for Yadavalli; it became deeply personal. Fear of the virus created divisions even within his own community. His colony, worried about exposure, barred him from entering the neighborhood. For months, he and his wife lived at their farm 90 kilometers away, making the long commute to the hospital every single day. Yet, despite the exhaustion and the risks, he remained steadfast. "I don't regret anything," he said. "I did what I could to help society and humanity." Then, with a laugh, he added, "I must have gotten COVID over 50 times!"

His unyielding dedication didn't just sustain him; it inspired his team. "When they saw me continuing to help, they asked themselves, 'If he can do it, why can't we?'" he said. This collective spirit of determination became a beacon of hope during the pandemic, underscoring the critical role healthcare professionals play in times of crisis.

For Yadavalli Subramanyam, these defining challenges were more than just tests of endurance—they were affirmations of his purpose. They taught him the power of perseverance, compassion, and leadership. Whether it was overcoming societal resistance in the early days of private healthcare or standing firm during the chaos of a global pandemic, Yadavalli's journey reaffirms his dedication to the healthcare field, demonstrating the impact of compassionate and purpose-driven leadership.

A Future Rooted in Purpose

Reflecting on the challenges of the COVID-19 pandemic, Yadavalli doesn't focus on the heartbreak or losses, though they remain etched in his memory. Instead, he feels a deep sense of fulfillment—of having been able to stand in the face of adversity and make a difference.

"For me, the reward lies in having been able to face those challenges and help people," he shared with quiet conviction. While the journey was marked by inevitable moments of loss—instances where lives could not be saved—it is the victories that shine brighter in his mind. "If we lost 10 people, but we helped 100 people live, that is the most rewarding thing. Nothing compares to that," he said, his words underscored by a deep sense of gratitude for the opportunity to serve.

As the world began its slow return to normalcy and life crept closer to what it once was, Yadavalli found himself reflecting on the lessons learned and the road ahead. His reintegration into the "ordinary world" wasn't about moving on but about recommitting to his purpose in healthcare with renewed energy and clarity. For Yadavalli, the pandemic was not just a crisis to survive—it was a call to action, a chance to realign with the values that had always driven him.

Looking forward, Yadavalli speaks with a quiet passion about inspiring others through his journey. "What I want to give across to the world," he explained, "is the understanding that perseverance, compassion, and the willingness to serve can bring about meaningful change—even in the face of extraordinary challenges." His words carry the weight of lived experience, the wisdom of someone who has stood at the crossroads of despair and hope and chosen to lead others toward the light. He believes that it's not just about treating the illness but also about understanding and alleviating the suffering of the patients.

But for Yadavalli, the journey doesn't end with overcoming the obstacles of yesterday. To him, those challenges are stepping stones—valuable lessons that serve as a foundation for building a more resilient, compassionate future. His vision is clear: to use his experiences not just to inspire but to create a ripple effect, where others too can find the strength to persevere and make a difference.

After achieving significant milestones in his journey, Yadavalli carries with him a philosophy rooted, yet again, in humility and respect—principles he believes are essential for reintegrating into everyday life, no matter how high one has risen.

"Humbleness doesn't cost anything, but it gives immense satisfaction," he says, his words carrying the wisdom of someone who has walked every rung of the ladder. For Yadavalli, humility is not just a personal virtue—it's a bridge that earns respect, strengthens relationships, and fosters a sense of connection, regardless of one's achievements or position.

Yadavalli's perspective on challenges and conflicts starkly reflects his ability to see opportunities where others might see only struggle. He doesn't view obstacles as setbacks but as catalysts for growth, creativity, and self-improvement. Looking back on his journey, he expresses gratitude for the experiences that have shaped him— whether it was starting as a ward boy, learning through each role, or leading at the helm as a CEO. "Every role in life is important," he says, a reminder that no contribution is too small, no position insignificant. His own story stands as proof of this belief.

To illustrate his philosophy, Yadavalli shares a story from the Indian epic 'Ramayan'—a comparison between Lord Ram and Ravana. "Despite Ravana's superior education, power, and resources, Ram prevailed because of his humility and respect for everyone," he explains. "When you're humble and respect everyone, the universe aligns to support you." For him, this story encapsulates a universal truth: arrogance may bring temporary success, but it is humility and respect that lead to enduring impact and harmony.

Yadavalli's message to the world is simple yet profound: embrace humility, honor every role, and recognize the value that each individual brings to the ecosystem. Whether it's a ward boy or a CEO, he believes that everyone contributes to the bigger picture, and it is this collective effort that drives progress. By practicing humility and respect, Yadavalli believes we can foster collaboration, spark growth, and cultivate a more profound sense of purpose in life.

Balancing Internal and External Worlds: A Key to Lifelong Growth

When asked what he has brought back from his journey so far, Yadavalli humbly states, "I don't think I have completed my journey." Instead, he emphasizes the ongoing nature of personal and professional growth, instilling a sense of hope and encouragement.

"The key to achieving anything lies in maintaining equilibrium between your internal and external worlds," he explains. Internal balance, encompassing emotional stability, self-awareness, and peace of mind, is as crucial as external balance, which involves effectively managing relationships, responsibilities, and external pressures.

Yadavalli, however, cautions against neglecting this balance, saying, "If you focus only on external balance while ignoring your internal harmony, you might achieve a heart attack, but not much else." This underscores the significance of self-care and the emphasis on emotional well-being alongside external achievements.

For him, this insight is not just a personal mantra but also a message for others: true success lies in finding harmony within oneself while working towards external goals. It is a continuous journey, not a destination, demanding constant introspection and adjustment.

Embracing Humility and Gratitude: A Journey of Continuous Learning

When reflecting on how his journey has shaped him, Yadavalli Subramanyam humbly acknowledges, "Every day, I learn a new perspective." Rather than marking a specific moment of change, he sees his growth as an ongoing process, with each day offering a new lesson.

Key to this journey has been the development of humility. He shares, "Every day, I become more humble," a testament to how personal growth and humility have become intertwined. Additionally, his experience has reinforced the fleeting nature of life, with the realization that "nothing is permanent" guiding him in both his professional and personal endeavors.

As Yadavalli reflects on the importance of gratitude, he states, "Every day I learn that in this short life, you need to respect others," emphasizing the importance of humility in relationships and leadership. He also acknowledges the foundational role of gratitude in his life, particularly toward his parents, mentors, and God's guidance, recognizing that "whatever you are today, it's because of them."

This continuous journey of learning and evolving will undoubtedly continue to impact his life moving forward as he applies these lessons of humility, gratitude, and respect to his personal and professional spheres.

For Yadavalli, the story of his journey is far from over—it's simply evolving into its next chapter, one shaped by a deep commitment to serving humanity and empowering others to do the same.

YADAVALLI SUBRAMANYAM, CO-AUTHOR

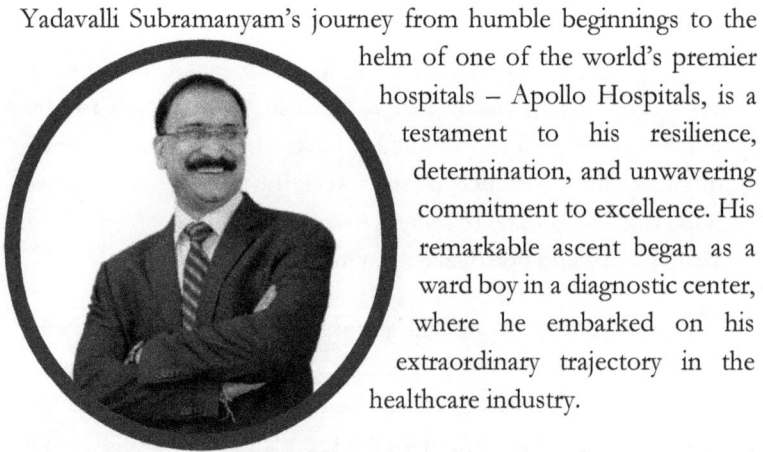

Yadavalli Subramanyam's journey from humble beginnings to the helm of one of the world's premier hospitals – Apollo Hospitals, is a testament to his resilience, determination, and unwavering commitment to excellence. His remarkable ascent began as a ward boy in a diagnostic center, where he embarked on his extraordinary trajectory in the healthcare industry.

Throughout his career, he encountered myriad challenges and obstacles, each serving as a steppingstone towards his ultimate destination. From the corridors of the diagnostic center to the boardrooms of Apollo Hospitals, he absorbed invaluable lessons at every turn, transforming setbacks into opportunities for growth and learning.

His journey to the pinnacles of management excellence began with his post-graduate studies in Management, laying the foundation for his illustrious career. However, his thirst for knowledge and quest for mastery led him to pursue numerous management courses from prestigious institutions around the globe.

From Berkeley in the USA to Singapore Management University, from the esteemed Indian Institutes of Management (IIM) in Ahmedabad and Bangalore to the Indian School of Business (ISB) and Kellogg University, his academic pedigree is nothing short of remarkable.

His holistic approach to management truly sets him apart, blending his expertise in marketing, operations, and strategy with a profound understanding of Indian and Western philosophies.

Delving deep into the realms of Indic philosophy, he sought wisdom from various gurus and rishis in India, enriching his perspective and imbuing his leadership with a unique blend of ancient wisdom and modern management principles.

Beyond his corporate role, his passion for sharing knowledge extends to the realm of academia. As a visiting faculty member at various prestigious institutes, he imparts his wealth of experience and insights to the next generation of leaders, shaping the future of management education.

7

THE LIFE, LEADERSHIP AND LEGACY OF DR. N.K. VENKATARAMANA

FROM VISION TO REALITY: CREATING BRAINS

Dr. N.K. Venkataramana 's journey is a story of evolution alongside a field that continues to inspire and challenge him. He shares a narrative of determination and passion, hoping to inspire others to pursue their dreams with the same fervor.

When Dr. Venkataramana first envisioned creating something extraordinary in the medical field, the idea felt both exhilarating and daunting. His goal was not merely to build a hospital; he sought to establish a center of excellence— a place where innovation met compassion and people from all walks of life could find solace in the face of illness. He wanted to create a sanctuary of healing that provided state-of-the-art medical care while prioritizing the human connection that defines the essence of medicine.

Before embarking on his remarkable journey as a doctor, Dr. Venkataramana 's life was much more straightforward, shaped by the realities of a small-town upbringing. His "normal" was grounded in a modest but significant existence, surrounded by a close-knit family emphasizing values, education, and perseverance.

Born in Tirupati, Andhra Pradesh, Dr. Venkataramana grew up in the historically rich town of Karvetinagaram. Hard work was not just encouraged—it was expected. His parents instilled in him a profound sense of discipline and a commitment to serving others. Education was a core focus during his early years, and though it wasn't glamorous, it laid the foundation for his lifelong passion for learning. His town, though modest, had its charm, including a palace steeped in history and Asia's second-largest stone-built pond, a marvel of ancient engineering. While he had no exposure to cutting-edge technology or vast resources, he relied on curiosity and a drive to understand how things worked—especially the human body. The local kings had generously donated the palace to serve as a school, and he was fortunate to study within its regal halls.

From a young age, Dr. Venkataramana was drawn to science, particularly biology. There was no question about his future—he dreamed of becoming a doctor. His daily routine was simple: wake up early, attend school, complete assignments, and spend time with family. Though his world felt limited, there was a sense of purpose in that limitation. His fascination with biology led him to spend hours reading science books, wondering how such intricate systems coexisted within the human body—and how they sometimes went wrong. These questions fueled his desire to study medicine.

Though resources were scarce and the idea of becoming a doctor seemed distant due to entrance exams, tuition fees, and the years of education required, Dr. Venkataramana held onto his dreams with unwavering determination. He knew that while he didn't start with many advantages, his hunger for knowledge and perseverance were strengths that couldn't be measured on paper.

The transition from his "normal" to the extraordinary journey in medicine was gradual. As he began his medical education, his worldview expanded dramatically. Moving from the confines of his small town to bustling cities, he encountered diverse people, ideas, and technologies. The journey was far from easy. It required immense sacrifice—not just from him but from his family, who supported him every step of the way. There were long nights of studying, sleepless hospital shifts, and moments of self-doubt. Yet, through it all, he found hope.

Reflecting on his beginnings, Dr. Venkataramana sees his early life as a grounding force that reminds him of where he started and helps keep him focused on his purpose. His upbringing taught him the value of human connection, humility, and the simple joys of life—qualities that became the foundation of his career as a doctor.

Dr. Venkataramana began his medical journey at Sri Venkateswara Medical College, a pivotal step that would shape the course of his life. During his studies, he became captivated by the brain, one of the human body's most enigmatic and complex organs. Its intricacies fascinated him, yet the difficulty of truly understanding it was challenging for students and his professors. While many of his peers avoided studying the brain, Dr. Venkataramana felt a magnetic pull to its complexities. This curiosity soon grew into a calling, and he decided to pursue a career in neurosurgery.

After completing his MBBS, Dr. Venkataramana furthered his education by enrolling in a neurosurgery course at NIMHANS in Bangalore, one of India's premier mental health and neuroscience institutions. His time there was transformative—academic rigor, hands-on experience, and interaction with experts deepened his knowledge of the brain. From the basics of brain anatomy to cutting-edge surgical techniques, he gradually developed a deep understanding of the organ he had become so fascinated by.

His neurosurgery training at NIMHANS was a rigorous but rewarding experience. Over five years, he delved into brain networks, biochemistry, clinical features, and surgical techniques, honing his skills in both diagnosis and surgery. By the time he completed his training, Dr. Venkataramana was fortunate to join the faculty at NIMHANS, where he continued to develop his expertise through research, teaching, and patient care.

As the years passed, Dr. Venkataramana witnessed firsthand how much the field of neurosurgery had evolved. When he began, neurosurgery in India was in its infancy. Medical schools didn't even have dedicated neurosurgery departments, and the field was met with skepticism. In those early days, treatments relied on rudimentary tools like X-rays and angiography, while surgical instruments were basic. However, over time, the introduction of technology like CT scans, MRIs, and the operating microscope revolutionized the field. Each advancement allowed for more precise diagnoses and treatments, transforming what was once considered a risky and uncertain specialty into a highly advanced discipline.

Despite these advances, neurosurgery remains a challenging field. The brain's complexity means surgeons must work with extreme precision, as even the slightest error can have profound consequences. However, the rewards of the field are immense. The ability to restore function and improve the quality of life for patients is deeply fulfilling.

Looking back, Dr. Venkataramana 's decision to pursue neurosurgery feels more like destiny than choice. The field was still evolving when he started, with only a few institutions in India offering training that could match global standards. His early challenges, particularly the depth of knowledge required to understand the brain truly—shaped his career. From that moment of humility, he immersed himself in studying the brain's structures and functions. He learned how to localize problems in the brain and develop precise diagnoses.

As the neurosurgery field advanced, so did Dr. Venkataramana 's understanding. The introduction of the operating microscope, followed by new technologies like endoscopy, required him to adapt and rethink how he viewed the brain. This constant evolution made neurosurgery challenging and exhilarating with each new tool and technique.

Through every challenge, Dr. Venkataramana 's passion for neurosurgery has only grown. His journey has been one of continuous learning, adaptation, and discovery, and he is proud to have been a part of the field's remarkable transformation. What once seemed impossible is now routine, and he continues to find fulfillment in pushing the boundaries of what neurosurgery can achieve.

Navigation systems, a groundbreaking innovation, have transformed the approach to surgeries. Borrowed from wartime technology—precisely the concept of precision bombing—they enabled surgeons to target precise areas of the brain without damaging surrounding tissue. This approach stood in stark contrast to the "carpet bombing" methods of the past. The ability to localize and navigate with such accuracy has opened once unimaginable possibilities. Today, even areas of the brain and spinal cord previously considered inaccessible can be operated on safely.

Despite these technological marvels, neurosurgery has retained its unpredictable and enigmatic nature. In the operating room, no two battles are ever the same. Each brain presents a new battlefield, every tumor a unique adversary, and every procedure a test of skill and adaptability. Neurosurgery leaves no room for complacency; it demands a balance between meticulous planning and on-the-spot improvisation.

No two surgeries are alike. Each brain, skull, and tumor presents distinct challenges, making neurosurgery a field devoid of monotony. It demands constant learning and preparation. While planning is critical, even the most carefully crafted strategies can falter. For this reason, having a contingency plan is essential. When unforeseen circumstances arise during a procedure, quick adaptation is vital to ensure the patient's safety.

The advent of intraoperative imaging techniques has been a revolutionary development. Real-time imaging allows surgeons to monitor the progress of surgery and make necessary adjustments, significantly enhancing precision and outcomes. However, even with advanced tools, maintaining a three-dimensional orientation of the brain remains one of neurosurgery's most critical challenges.

This challenge infuses the field with vitality, turning it from a routine discipline into a lifelong journey of discovery. Neurosurgery is dynamic, ever-changing, and alive. Each advancement brings a renewed curiosity and a drive to push beyond the horizon of possibility. Every new case is a reminder that, amidst the familiar, there is always more to learn, master, and achieve.

The field's continuous evolution brings fulfillment through the opportunity to learn and grow. Each technological advancement and each unique case pushes the boundaries of what is achievable. Today, even the most complex conditions, such as deep-seated brain tumors or intricate spinal cord abnormalities, can be addressed with remarkable success.

As the field advances, it is essential to look beyond surgery itself. One neurosurgeon, in particular, found his research interest rooted in improving brain function and rehabilitating patients with neurological disabilities. One of his most exciting areas of exploration has been regenerative medicine, including using stem cells to restore brain function. The goal of combining surgical precision with innovations in rehabilitation and assistive technology has been to enhance patients' quality of life. Neurological disabilities are profoundly impactful, and finding ways to help individuals regain independence remains a driving force behind his work.

This broader vision reflects the journey he has taken in neurosurgery. This journey began with a humble understanding of the brain and became a lifelong pursuit of unraveling its mysteries. Each milestone in the field marks how far neurosurgery has come while underscoring how much remains to be discovered. The field has evolved dramatically, transitioning from rudimentary tools to cutting-edge technologies and from limited knowledge to an era of precision and breakthroughs. Yet, the brain remains as fascinating as ever, an enduring mystery waiting to be unraveled.

What began as an intimidating subject for this surgeon became his life's work and passion. He remains deeply grateful to the mentors who guided him, the colleagues who challenged him, and the patients who entrusted him with their lives. Each played a pivotal role in his journey, teaching him the value of persistence, humility, and the relentless pursuit of excellence.

Neurosurgery is not merely a profession; it is a calling. It demands dedication, resilience, and a profound sense of responsibility. Yet, it offers unparalleled rewards—the opportunity to change lives, heal, and advance humanity's understanding of one of nature's most complex creations. For this neurosurgeon, these rewards have made every challenge, sleepless night, and moment of doubt worthwhile.

When he stepped into the field, his passion for neurosurgery was unrelenting. Each surgery deepened his fascination, every discovery opened new doors, and every challenge underscored the untapped potential within the field. He became acutely aware of systemic gaps while dedicating himself to surgeries, research, and teaching. Despite India's abundance of brilliant minds and potential, he was frustrated by the lack of resources and infrastructure. This frustration became the seed of an idea that would ultimately lead him down his career's most ambitious and transformative path.

Publishing papers, speaking at conferences, and exchanging ideas with global pioneers exposed him to groundbreaking advancements in neurosurgery in countries like Germany, Japan, and the United States. Witnessing these innovations left him inspired but also profoundly aware of the disparity between India and the rest of the world. Financial, infrastructural, and systemic barriers continued to hold the country back. While global knowledge became more accessible through the internet and collaborations, translating that knowledge into practice in India was no small feat.

His journey took him through numerous hospitals, beginning with NIMHANS, where his foundations were built. At NIMHANS, the immense clinical load and relentless pace tested his endurance but also molded him into the professional he is today. Over time, he transitioned to private institutions, gaining valuable experience, establishing departments, and pursuing his vision. However, he encountered recurring challenges, such as management changes and conflicting institutional priorities, which hindered his ability to achieve long-term goals. These limitations led him to the realization that to bring his vision to life indeed, he needed the freedom to build something of his own.

The turning point came during his time at NIMHANS, following a particularly harrowing night on call. From midnight until dawn, a steady stream of patients arrived—victims of road traffic accidents. Each case was fatal, involving catastrophic injuries and alcohol consumption. The experience was profoundly unsettling. Why were these lives lost? What could be done to prevent such tragedies?

This realization began his broader mission: to address systemic failures and improve emergency care in India. He founded an NGO, the Comprehensive Trauma Consortium, launching Bangalore's first free ambulance service long before the advent of the 108 system. Immersing himself in the logistics of emergency care, he observed inefficiencies in accident handling, lack of coordination, and inadequate infrastructure. These challenges spurred him to action and strengthened his resolve to create meaningful change.

This gap led Dr. Venkataramana to explore regenerative medicine, specifically stem cell research. The idea of neural regeneration—helping the brain heal—captivated him. While humanity may not yet have the ability to recreate the brain, he believed in the power of preserving its function and improving patients' quality of life. This research became a cornerstone of BRAINS, the institute he founded. Once again, he relied on the support and expertise of collaborators who shared his vision.

At its core, BRAINS is about more than just treating neurological conditions—it represents a new standard for neuroscience in India. From neurocritical care to rehabilitation, the institute aims to address every aspect of a patient's journey. This holistic approach is innovative and essential in a country where access to comprehensive care is often fragmented.

Dr. Venkataramana has always believed that keeping the brain healthy is the key to overall well-being. In his view, if the brain functions optimally, it can better manage the body's needs than any external intervention. This philosophy drives much of the work at BRAINS, from developing new treatments to creating rehabilitation programs that empower patients to live independently.

Looking back, his journey is filled with challenges, breakthroughs, and an unwavering belief in the power of dreams. For Dr. Venkataramana , creating BRAINS was not just about filling a gap in Indian healthcare but proving that world-class excellence could be achieved at home. Every step of this journey reinforced his conviction that anything is possible with the right combination of passion, collaboration, and determination.

Today, BRAINS is a testament to what can be accomplished when one refuses to settle for mediocrity. It is more than an institute;

it symbolizes hope, innovation, and the relentless pursuit of excellence in neuroscience. Dr. Venkataramana 's story is far from over. His journey continues, fueled by the same passion that set him on this path decades ago. Together with his team, he envisions a future where no challenge is too great and no dream too ambitious.

Every journey begins with gratitude, and this is no exception. Dr. Venkataramana attributes his success to the incredible teachers who shared their knowledge, inspired him, and ignited his curiosity. They laid the foundation for the person and professional he has become, and their wisdom continues to guide him. He is equally indebted to the circle of friends and colleagues who stood by him—people from diverse walks of life who enriched his vision and offered support in countless ways.

Among them are international peers who broadened his horizons, educators who sharpened his understanding, and professionals—business leaders, chartered accountants, and government officials—who lent their expertise and encouragement. Their unwavering belief in his dream was instrumental in bringing it to life.

With their guidance and support, he set out to build something extraordinary: a center of excellence in neuroscience. The journey has been gradual, often challenging, but deeply fulfilling. Slowly, systems and processes that reflected his vision were implemented.

Yet, a vision is never static—it grows, evolves, and demands more with each step forward. As he laid the foundation for world-class care, the question evolved from what had been achieved to what could be aspired to next. The possibilities felt limitless, and the responsibility to harness them extraordinary. This led him to focus on improving outcomes and reimagining how neuroscience care could be delivered, from the speed of emergency response to the depth of care during recovery.

The goal was to deliver world-class services, and while significant strides have been made, there is still much to accomplish. The institute aims to amplify its services, integrate cutting-edge technologies, and embrace emerging sub-specialties in the field. One key initiative has been implementing the "golden hour" concept, emphasizing the critical importance of timely intervention in medical emergencies. Additionally, the institute works to enhance the rehabilitation process for patients, ensuring their recovery is as holistic and practical as possible.

For Dr. Venkataramana , the pursuit of excellence does not end at the bedside; it extends to the frontier of discovery. He realized early on that redefining neuroscience care required contributing to knowledge, pushing boundaries, and innovating solutions to pressing challenges. Research became a bridge between vision and reality—a way to turn groundbreaking ideas into life-changing outcomes. His focus has been translational research, bridging the gap between laboratory findings and clinical applications. The goal is simple yet profound: to turn scientific discoveries into tangible medical solutions.

One such challenge has been spinal cord injuries. A damaged spinal cord often means irreversible consequences, leaving patients with little hope of recovery. To Dr. Venkataramana , this is unacceptable. He and his team work tirelessly to explore ways to regenerate or reconnect damaged spinal cords, allowing patients to reclaim their lives.

Another area of focus is malignant brain tumors. Despite advancements in medical science, some forms of brain cancer remain stubbornly resistant to treatment. These challenges, though daunting, fuel his determination. The research seeks breakthroughs to turn seemingly insurmountable obstacles into solvable problems.

Yet, research and innovation alone aren't enough to build an enduring legacy. Transforming ideas into reality requires resilience and vision. Creating an institution of this magnitude was never going to be easy. Financial constraints, logistical complexities, and ideological clashes have marked the journey. However, Dr. Venkataramana saw challenges not as barriers but as architects of ingenuity and growth. Each hurdle became a lesson in perseverance and the collective strength of a team bound by a shared purpose.

As BRAINS grows, the need to stay true to its mission becomes even more pressing. The institute is committed to world-class care and ensuring every patient who walks through its doors receives compassionate, innovative care tailored to their needs. This requires constant evolution—adapting to new technologies, integrating emerging specialties, and expanding capabilities in rehabilitation and research.

Growth, as Dr. Venkataramana often emphasizes, is never a solitary journey. Behind every step forward is the strength of collaboration and a shared dream. From the beginning, he has been surrounded by individuals who believed in his vision as much as he did. Their financial, technical, and moral contributions have been this journey's lifeblood. This network of collaborators has been vital in building not just the physical infrastructure of the institute but also its ethos. Together, they have created a space that is more than a hospital or research center: it is a community dedicated to advancing neuroscience and improving lives.

Inspired by the efficient systems he had seen in Germany, Dr. Venkataramana sought to replicate them. He equipped ambulances with essential medical devices and introduced training programs to create a cadre of skilled paramedics. These individuals, often science graduates, were trained in critical techniques like airway management, IV line insertion, bleeding control, and the ABCs of emergency care: Airway, Breathing, and Circulation.

One of the most critical ideas he implemented was the golden hour concept. The first hour following a medical emergency, especially a head injury, is crucial, as timely intervention can mean the difference between life and death—or between recovery and permanent disability. Dr. Venkataramana had witnessed countless cases where preventable secondary complications claimed lives. He designed a system to address these issues head-on, with a centralized control room, a single emergency number, and wireless communication integrated with monitoring systems. Ambulances were strategically stationed across the city to minimize response times. The impact was immediate and profound.

Traffic congestion, inadequate roads, and the lack of dedicated ambulance lanes presented challenges. However, through persistence and collaboration, the program succeeded. By 2001, nearly 22% of accident victims in the region had died before reaching the hospital. Over the years, that figure was reduced to 5%. While the achievement was significant, sustaining such programs required extensive resources. Eventually, the government stepped in with initiatives like 108. While this was a step forward, Dr. Venkataramana acknowledges that India's emergency care systems still have much room for improvement.

Time is the most critical factor in saving lives, especially in the case of head injuries. Dr. Venkataramana firmly believes that the proper care delivered at the right time and place can prevent death and disability, reduce hospital costs, and vastly improve the quality of life for patients. For him, the golden hour is not just a concept but a promise—a commitment to valuing human life above all else.

The journey to revolutionize emergency care and advanced neurological treatment under his leadership has been marked by significant challenges. While many obstacles have been overcome through innovation and resourcefulness, the sustainability of such initiatives remains a constant battle.

One of the most pressing issues Dr. Venkataramana has faced is scaling up operations, particularly in ambulances, manpower, and technology. Advanced imaging and surgical equipment essential for neurosurgery often come at exorbitant costs, driven by import dependence and an unfavorable rupee-to-dollar exchange rate. While developed countries enjoy seamless integration of the latest technologies, he and his team have had to innovate and optimize with minimal resources. Tailoring solutions to local constraints has required meticulous effort, yet compromising on critical technology was never an option for him, as the consequences would have been dire.

To address these limitations, Dr. Venkataramana has worked tirelessly to secure funding, streamline resources, and sustain high-quality operations while maintaining affordability. Though insurance penetration has improved in India, challenges persist in balancing costs with quality. It remains a delicate, ongoing process.

Another critical issue he has championed is raising awareness about neurological health. Misconceptions, particularly in rural areas, continue to hinder timely medical intervention. Epilepsy, for example, is often misunderstood as a possession or an astrological phenomenon. Traditional remedies are often pursued exclusively, delaying essential medical care.

Dr. Venkataramana has also observed that outdated practices frequently hinder progress in treating strokes, a primary neurological concern. Many individuals still rely on practices such as massages instead of seeking immediate medical attention. Similarly, spinal surgery misconceptions result in advanced paralysis cases, and treatable conditions like pituitary tumors are often neglected until they cause severe complications like blindness.

To combat these myths, Dr. Venkataramana launched a monthly magazine, Brain Voice, published in both English and Kannada, to educate the public on neurological diseases, treatments, and advancements. This magazine, a labor of love, has been running successfully for over five years. He has also utilized TV interviews, professional lectures, and continuing medical education (CME) programs to raise awareness among the public and healthcare professionals.

In recent years, he has also turned his attention to rare neurological diseases, which are often misdiagnosed or dismissed as psychiatric issues due to their complexity and subtle presentations. He established a Rare Neurological Disease Clinic to address this, providing a comprehensive evaluation and management platform. The clinic ensures no condition is prematurely dismissed by meticulously studying early, often overlooked symptoms.

Despite these hurdles, Dr. Venkataramana remains inspired by his witnessed progress. His efforts to demystify neurological health, improve accessibility to treatment, and adopt cutting-edge technology demonstrate an unwavering commitment to his cause. Challenges persist in logistics, funding, and awareness, but the strides made continue to offer hope.

Dr. Venkataramana is deeply committed to ensuring that every individual, regardless of socioeconomic status, has access to world-class neurological care. His journey is one of continuous innovation, collaboration, and unrelenting dedication. Through education, technological advancements, and community engagement, he aims to bridge the gap between potential and reality in neurological care.

One of his early challenges was integrating advanced technology into his systems. He understood that embracing the latest innovations was non-negotiable to remain at the forefront of medical care. However, acquiring and implementing these tools came with a steep learning curve and significant costs.

Beyond technology, he recognized early on that the heart of any successful institution lies in its people. Identifying and recruiting skilled medical professionals requires a discerning eye and an understanding of their qualifications and passion for healing.

For Dr. Venkataramana , the journey of building a healthcare institution felt akin to nurturing a delicate ecosystem. Each component—technology, processes, people, and quality standards—must work harmoniously. In the early days, it seemed like a never-ending process of creating, implementing, and refining systems. Daily challenges ranged from infection control measures to raising awareness about the hospital and ensuring operational efficiency.

As he reflects on four decades in the medical profession, Dr. Venkataramana acknowledges that his most valuable lesson is that passion is the foundation of this field. His advice to aspiring medical professionals is simple: choose this path only if you have a deep, enduring passion. The field demands not only hard work but also genuine compassion for others.

As he sees it, this compassion operates on two levels: toward the subject and the patient. A love for the subject fuels the desire to constantly learn, adapt to new technologies, and improve skills. Compassion for patients ensures that every effort is directed toward achieving the best outcomes, even in challenging circumstances.

Dr. Venkataramana has also become deeply invested in the intersection of technology and healthcare. He sees innovation as the key to reducing the cost of medical treatments and making them more accessible. However, many advanced tools, such as MRI machines, remain prohibitively expensive due to their reliance on imports. He emphasizes the urgent need for indigenous innovation and robust systems to support research and development in India.

Reflecting on his journey, Dr. Venkataramana acknowledges the privilege of engaging with humanity at its most vulnerable and authentic moments. For him, medicine is both a science and an art—requiring empathy, intuition, and creativity.

In addition to his work as a surgeon and clinical care provider, he remains fascinated by the human brain, not only from a medical perspective but also from metaphysical and spiritual dimensions. He finds inspiration in ancient scriptures that offer profound insights into human consciousness. By bridging past wisdom with present-day science, Dr. Venkataramana envisions unlocking the untapped potential to improve the human condition.

The future of medicine deeply excites Dr. Venkataramana . He believes that technological advances, from robotics to artificial intelligence, can revolutionize patient care. However, he emphasizes that these tools will complement, not replace, the human touch. He believes medicine will always require skilled professionals who combine expertise and empathy.

Looking ahead, Dr. Venkataramana remains focused on creating efficient and compassionate systems. Whether it is through designing patient-friendly hospitals, fostering innovation, or improving processes, his commitment is to ensure that healthcare remains a beacon of hope for all.

To those embarking on a similar journey, Dr. Venkataramana offers this advice: prioritize clinical excellence, but do not overlook the importance of research, innovation, and knowledge-sharing. He encourages embracing technology while staying grounded in the humanity that defines the medical profession. Above all, he urges approaching the field with passion, compassion, and an unwavering dedication to making a meaningful difference.

For Dr. Venkataramana , medicine is not merely a profession but a calling. He sees it as a force that can transform lives—not just the lives of patients but also those who practice it. His journey has been one of growth, learning, and service, and he reflects on it with immense gratitude, knowing he would not trade it for anything in the world.

DR. N.K. VENKATARAMANA, CO-AUTHOR

Dr. N.K. Venkataramana is a distinguished neurosurgeon with over 35 years of experience and thousands of operations performed. As the Founder Chairman and Director of Neurosciences at BRAINS Hospitals in Bangalore, India, he has been at the forefront of neurological and neurosurgical advancements. Dr. Venkataramana's illustrious career includes pioneering efforts in neuro-endoscopy, deep brain stimulation, and stem cell research for neuro-regeneration.

He has held prestigious positions such as Vice Chairman at BGS Global Hospitals, Director of Neurosciences at Manipal Hospital, and Assistant Professor of Neurosurgery at NIMHANS. His contributions to pediatric neurosurgery, cerebrovascular surgery, neuro-endoscopy, and neuronal regeneration have been widely recognized.

An accomplished academic and researcher, Dr. Venkataramana has published numerous articles in leading medical journals and authored several books and chapters on neurosurgery. He is also the Editor-in-Chief of "Brain Voice". He has been integral to multiple professional societies, including the Asian Australian Society for

Pediatric Neurosurgery and the International Federation of Neuro-endoscopy.

Dr. Venkataramana's innovative work and dedication to advancing neurosurgical care have earned him numerous accolades, including the Karnataka Rajyotsava Award, Times Healthcare Legend Award, and the Sir C.V. Raman Birth Centenary Award presented by the Prime Minister of India. His commitment to trauma care led to the establishment of the Comprehensive Trauma Consortium, which significantly improved emergency medical services in Bangalore.

For more information, visit http://www.brainshospital.com.

8

THE LIFE, LEADERSHIP AND LEGACY OF ATMA GUNUPUDI

EMBRACING THE CONFLICT WITHIN

Shifting into an entirely different field, especially one that is still emerging with no expected trajectory, is difficult. It's also a decision that people around you might doubt and question whether it's really worth it. These decisions are tough to make; it's an unavoidable gamble that something you want to invest in or a line of business you might want to take up might seem too unpromising to others.

In times like that, you look to people who have trusted themselves and pushed on into the field they had such high hopes for, taking reassurance from their triumphs. You look to people who shut out the naysayers and trudged on till they reached their goal.

You look to people like Atma Gunupudi.

Gunupudi always had a fire in him, which was made further obvious to him as he entered the workforce. Starting his work in 2004, even with his first job and even though he had certain tasks outlined for him in his job description, Gunupudi still found himself gravitating towards the intricacies of business work. About how a business truly runs underneath all the typical employee management.

When he shifted into business and operations management, he found that fire growing bigger, drawing him closer to businesses' "bottom lines." How the money was being made, how it was being spent, how could they save on spending while increasing revenue—these were the questions that tumbled around in Gunupudi's mind.

He'd always been good at handling leadership roles, even when younger, participating in several extracurricular activities and even becoming a leader during his university days. Perhaps that was when he started to realize that influencing and leading people came naturally to him. He managed to demonstrate this easily during the early chapters of his career. By 2011-12, he was handling global charters with more than 100 people, considering that the true beginning of his leadership journey was when he took up the role of Global Head for Escalation Management at Salesforce. But before that definite start, he'd found himself picking up relevant skills, going out of his comfort zone, and solving problems outside his job description to gain more understanding of the field he was so interested in. So, in a way, Gunupudi's life before stepping into leadership has simply been a preparation for that step—a drive that the readers will definitely understand.

The Moment of Truth

People often discuss "the moment," a recollection that everyone, from fans to non-fans to haters, wishes to know, the exact pinpoint memory of a "moment" when the person knew they were stepping down their destined path. Do such moments truly exist?

Gunupudi thought about it, the realization that there is a weight to the impact you create, whether as a single person or while working in an organization. That got him thinking about things like the compounding effect of the work that anyone does or even the nonlinear growth of the firm. What truly pushed him to pursue his leadership career was understanding the multiplier effect and the unfolding of all these metrics. To understand the optimal management of, say, 100 people, who each work 8 hours a day, which means a total of 800 hours of labor in a single day. He was immediately drawn to how 800 hours could be made efficient enough to generate an output of 1600 hours of work. He also recognized that an upcoming generation of young workers wanted to see that acceleration and ended up burning candles on both ends, working ridiculously long hours even though there were only 24 in a day. All of these realizations stoked the fire in him, incentivizing his decision to turn into leadership.

Once he reached a point where his career could not be made more efficient or enhanced further, he sought out other problems away from business operations that may help, finding problems closer to customers and the bottom line, triggering a new fire in him.

Doubts and Getting Around Them

Second-guessing yourself and having doubts about your choices are common, though many assume that the accomplished are untouched by them. Atma Gunupudi, when discussing the possibility of doubts, emphatically asserted the reality of his own doubts. In fact, he revealed the unyielding nature of doubts, and it was their nature to creep up on every decision and turn he took in life. Every time he undertook a new challenge and a new landscape to work on, Gunupudi experienced discomfort, doubt, and restlessness plaguing him through every beginning. But after several rounds of these emotions, he decided to change his viewpoint. The feelings of unease and doubt will crop up regardless of what venture he undertakes. Then, the only solution is to embrace those feelings, become comfortable with them, and examine the roots. He could find a way to assuage the doubts by bringing out practice efficiency or creative problem-solving until he was more comfortable on this new path. The more he employed this technique with himself, the more capable he would become in dealing with the doubts. If the doubts popped up every time he was outside his comfort zone, then he developed a mechanism where the simplest way to not be affected would be to accept and become comfortable even with that doubt and restlessness.

If becoming comfortable with restlessness and dealing with it could be called post-doubt care, then there definitely exists pre-doubt care—an act or interaction that can provide reassurance before the doubts crop up, namely, speaking to mentors and guides.

During the formative stages of his career, when he joined Salesforce in 2010, Gunupudi was surrounded by phenomenal leaders who pushed for creative problem-solving and active questioning of the status quo. He gratefully mentions Mr. Atul Nanda, Head of Support at Salesforce, who greatly influenced this thought process when working there. Another he mentions is Mr. Chandra Cherukutota, VP of Engineering, who, despite being an engineer by trade, was very interested in improving customer value and understanding customer satisfaction. That was where he internalized the vital philosophy of not focusing only on the creation of products but also on understanding their use and the scope for improvement. Gunupudi quotes Mr Cherukutota as a source of many of these learnings.

Doubt always presents itself as the rock you trip over as you turn onto a new road, but there are other challenges that often hinder people from growth. Gunupudi, now a mentor himself, has managed to master the correct attitude to adapt to face these roadblocks. The initial challenges he noted have always been connected to reputation, not just in himself but also in the environment. As a believer in "quick wins, easy wins," he stresses the fact that a problem is never impossible to solve. It works better if you tackle smaller tasks first, doing them well and quickly and presenting them as proof of your skills before slowly making your way up to bigger, more complicated problems. Those smaller issues help you understand your position and whether you have the ideal temperament for the scope of work. If the basics are solid and unfailing, the next step is to divide the seemingly enormous tasks into small, digestible steps.

There is no "big bang" approach to things, Gunupudi insists. Those who succeed like that are extremely lucky, and luck is not easy to come by. Instead, most rely on hard work and slowly making their way up the ladder. It becomes a matter of patience, resilience, and a hint of something as simple as belief in yourself.

When ruminating over the nature of his allies and adversaries over the years, Gunupudi revealed interesting insight into how he perceived those relationships. In his eyes, allies changed based on the problem, environment, and even country. And while he's had personal adversaries, many times, it didn't come from a personal point of view. Often, when you challenge or speak out against the status quo, those who have become comfortable with it will move against you. There were definitely people who didn't want to see him grow or saw the growth as a hindrance to their own growth, but he makes it a point to acknowledge how situational adversaries and allies exist and how those relations can melt when that situation itself disappears. He adds that he's even had certain adversaries turn into well-appreciated allies. There are two outcomes of this, as he shares. The first is that, due to your genuine hard work in the right direction, the market will slowly tilt in your direction, allowing you to leave your adversaries in the dust. Additionally, as you commit to this job, some people will slowly start to recognize that you're showing results and are also genuine in your attempt to hear out their concerns and address them with your efforts. This slowly allows them to turn from adversaries into allies, sticking with you for the long run.

There are other challenges he faced during his journey, including resource constraints and time allotment challenges. These are challenges that don't cease after the company reaches a certain level or accomplishes a certain goal but rather reappear again and again. Additionally, when expanding internationally, he had to deal with cultural changes that came with market dynamics.

However, through all these trials, Gunupudi learned how to employ his perseverance and creativity to come up with ideas and fresh solutions to problems. Some challenges are proportionate to the size of the goal, and a bottom line that should be kept in mind is being comfortable with the challenge. After a while, it becomes normal.

Overcoming these challenges is always said to bring a distinct feeling of relief and reward. The advice that Gunupudi offers here is to take the time to celebrate. While it no doubt makes for good PR, the true motive behind these parties is to allow appreciation of the team that worked so hard to contribute to the success. Celebrate everyone's success with your allies. It makes sure to foster motivation and good feelings between the team. After celebrating, he also advised reflecting on what success means for me and what it means going forward. By re-implementing this time and time again, Gunupudi saw relations and bonds flourish for a long time.

Slipping Back Into The Everyday

Shocks will come to you, whether through a win or loss. Gunupudi, who observed successful people, mentions their ability to return to their norms extremely quickly. It involves a mindset that doesn't get carried away with success and instead snaps back into the hardworking routine the next day. It could be as simple as waking up at like 5 am and having your coffee at 5.30, going to bed at 10, like whatever that normal is; I think some people have normal in their lifestyle, some people have normal in their environment, like the houses or the colonies that they stay in, but whatever that is, I think number one, even before you get to answer of this question, you should be very cognizant of what normal is for you. It's the same logic as military people shifting back to their routines no matter what has happened the previous day. It becomes important to stick to that routine of "normal" as if to come back to the equilibrium of your life, not allowing yourself to get drunk off victory or drown in defeat. This is why Gunupudi kindly suggests taking a little time, maybe the day, to immerse yourself in the feeling of the conclusion, go to bed, and then wake up again in your norm, ready to tackle another day.

And Moving Forward

There are four exact impacts that Gunupudi notes from his leadership journey.

The first is his confidence. Understanding that no problem is fundamentally unsolvable can do wonders for your confidence, a fact that Gunupudi heavily emulates. There can be several things to solve, maybe an issue of bad planning, incomplete learning, or something else. But a rooted understanding that there is nothing that you can't learn for the first time, and no problem can remain "unsolved," shapes a better mindset towards issues.

Second, learning that being humble works. Gunupudi discusses how the more open he became to feedback and the more humility he presented, the more successful he found myself becoming. People's thoughts, whether criticism or advice, can always help whether in big ways or small ways.

The third learning, was that goals will always keep changing. Having published his book in 2024, "The Customer Success

Flywheel: Recurring Revenue Growth: A Practical Guide," he realized that it became old news soon enough. As he grows, his goals change, and success changes as well. This allowed him to look more towards constantly challenging and furthering himself, which is why he is currently pursuing his PhD in ISB.

The fourth fact he mentioned was the need to tweak his surroundings appropriately. Whether it's physical surroundings or the people that stand around him, maintaining an environment that supports him the way he needs it became incredibly important. When it comes to friends, family, and well-wishers gather people who believe in you and who are motivating you to do more. The more you hear people say no to you, the more self-talk you start, and then there is a negative spiral you should avoid.

Finally, from a tactical and financial perspective, having a "war chest" is a choice you would never regret. He talks about how the confidence that a war chest and the amount of savings you have for a rainy day help you become unhindered by the inconsistencies in the external environment if you have a good war chest for the inconsistencies in the external intellectual market.

Atma Gunupudi's Advice List

1. **Understand your Grand Goals and break them into bite-sized, achievable goals.** What do you need to do today? It also goes to building discipline, however, more often than not, discipline is not the question; it's about planning and trying to convert a bite-size goal, which will be more palatable and easier to manage.

2. **Celebrate your wins.** In order to not get bogged down by a continuous workflow, get burnt out, or face dissatisfaction from fellow workers, take the time to spread appreciation and celebration. These things don't last for too long, often

only lasting a night. Seize that night (as opposed to seizing the day) and throw good vibes and compliments around to rejuvenate everyone and energize them for upcoming projects.

3. **Build teams.** Have teams to work with you in the various spheres you're involved with, whether it's social, personal, relationship-based, and so on. This helps you create productive or comforting groups that you can lean on and motivate you.

4. **Before you leap, have a steady beat out.** Whether it's a war chest, a safety net, or a plan B, make sure you're not going into anything blind and won't suffer too hard if any mistake crops up. Don't let a lack of cushioning be the reason you don't get to experiment or try out new alleys.

ATMA GUNUPUDI, CO-AUTHOR

With a rich and extensive background in customer success spanning diverse industries and various customer success (CS) functions, Atma Gunupudi has undoubtedly made a lasting imprint on the field. Throughout his career, Atma has dedicated a significant portion of his professional journey to mastering the intricacies of customer success discipline, earning him high praise for his deep expertise in the domain.

Currently serving as the leader of all post-sales customer-facing teams at MoEngage, Atma showcases his adeptness in managing an impressive portfolio comprising thousands of eclectic customers. His strategic initiatives and adept leadership have consistently driven substantial revenue, amounting to over a hundred million throughout his career trajectory. Atma's ability to navigate complex customer landscapes and deliver tangible results underscores his exceptional talent in the realm of customer success.

Furthermore, Atma's influence transcends geographical boundaries, as evidenced by his track record of providing invaluable counsel to numerous CXOs and CS heads across different countries. His insights and guidance have been instrumental in both establishing and fortifying robust customer success functions, contributing to organizational growth and sustainability on a global scale.

9

THE LIFE, LEADERSHIP AND LEGACY OF RAJ GOPAL

THE TRANSFORMATIONAL CHANGE

"Don't be afraid to give up the good to go for the great."

– John D. Rockefeller

Behind every trailblazer lies a story of perseverance, growth, and an unwavering dedication to creating lasting change. Raj Gopal's journey is no different, yet far from ordinary. An extraordinary path defined by resilience, a relentless drive to innovate, and an unwavering belief in the power of collaboration. From his early ventures in entrepreneurship to his current role as a leader in the tech industry, Raj's life and career have been powerful demonstrations of the transformative power of grit and vision, inspiring us all to embrace resilience and the power of collaboration in our own journeys.

From the very beginning, Raj knew one thing for certain. While he wasn't always sure about the specifics—what he would do, how he would do it, or even whether he was just following the tech/IT wave like everyone else—he still jumped on board. But unlike the many who simply rode the trend, Raj approached the technology landscape of the early '90s with the curiosity of a wanderer, exploring every opportunity it had to offer.

One thing remained constant: he always knew he wanted his career to culminate in an entrepreneurial venture. Even in the early stages, he ventured into entrepreneurship, carving out new paths and showcasing the ingenuity that would define his leadership style. However, it was his transition into the technology sector that truly cemented his impact. By embracing rapid innovation, Raj not only thrived but also played a pivotal role in driving organizational growth, shaping the future of companies in an increasingly competitive landscape. Over the years, he has contributed to the success of several tech enterprises, always with a focus on creating solutions that drive meaningful change.

For Raj, leadership is not defined by accolades but by the ability to empower others, inspire change, and tackle challenges head-on. His leadership philosophy is built on service, *empathy, and resilience*—qualities that have guided him through every phase of his journey. Raj's ability to unite diverse teams, fostering collaboration and a culture of innovation, has been a driving force behind his success. His impact stretches far beyond organizational growth; it is evident in how he encourages continuous learning, adapts to change, and leads by example.

Early Life and Career Beginnings

A native of Bangalore, Raj grew up in the city and followed the most conventional paths until he didn't. Well, conventional because the road he set out on was a more downtrodden one (one that many had walked down)—he completed his schooling, thereafter, his college education, and finally stepped into the professional sphere.

The IT boom was at its peak when he graduated, and like moths to a flame, everyone set out to be swept by the tech wave that had just hit India.

However, since Raj was determined to set up his own venture, he chose not to conform to traditional roles. Here, the road started getting a little grassy, a path few dared to take. Since his interest and inclination were toward the business operation end of an organization, Raj consciously decided to delve into aspects beyond the technical ones. He focused on marketing, business development, pre-sales, and sales in the 25 years he spent. Roles that extended beyond what his formal education had prepared him for.

Now, having completed his 33rd year in the industry, looking back, Raj feels a sense of fulfillment, having led and still leading a journey that spans the entire spectrum of IT. Seeing the landscape evolve from its nascent stages when the IT wave hit India, Raj described the early days of his career as something that seemed to me like the difference between a vintage car and a modern electric vehicle. "When I started my career in 1991, it was a time when selling computers was more about educating people on what they were and how they worked. Back then, computers weren't as commonplace as they are today. We were dealing with Intel 286 processors—ancient by today's standards—paired with CGA monitors that had limited clarity. If you remember the old railway station booking counters with those flickering screens, that's the kind of technology we worked with. Memory was minimal, and the machines were slow, but they were revolutionary at the time."

From there, he moved on to networking, thereafter delving into software and later into mainframes. His journey continued through telecom software and product engineering, eventually leading him to embedded product design. His career has always been driven by a desire to explore new frontiers rather than just settle into a comfort zone. He has rarely taken on roles where he could rely on his past connections or leverage his network or previous experiences. Instead, steadfastly, he constantly sought new challenges, whether it was a different geographic location where he knew no one or a domain entirely unfamiliar to him. This continuous learning and adaptability have been key to his success in the ever-evolving tech industry.

But like in every other industrial landscape, the markets tend to be polynomial. Not every transition was smooth, and some roles came with significant hurdles. However, through it all, Raj remained committed to growth, reinvention, and embracing the unknown.

"Success, in my view, isn't just about how well we do in each assignment but about the continuous learning and evolution that come with it," Raj's words deeply resonated. Success has always been about perseverance—whether you push through challenges or succumb to them. Life isn't about scoring a six on every ball; sometimes, you need to step back, let a few go, or take a single before you build momentum again. The key is to recognize that setbacks are just phases, and as long as you enjoy the journey, you'll find a way forward.

With this mindset, he spent about 12 years working abroad, focusing on business development. His first move was to Australia—a region he knew little about at the time. Later, he transitioned to Germany, not just changing locations but stepping into a new cultural and linguistic landscape altogether. Adapting to these challenges became second nature, and he thrived on the learning curve that came with each shift. When asked how he managed to start from scratch each time and still prosper, Raj said, "I have always believed that struggle is essential for growth. By intentionally taking on complex roles and working in unfamiliar environments, I ensured that my journey remained dynamic and engaging. Without that sense of challenge, corporate life can become monotonous, and I was determined to keep evolving."

The Return to India and the Entrepreneurial Leap

Despite his years abroad, settling there was never the plan. Raj always knew he would return to India, and when he did, he joined Siemens. Once again, it was a completely new domain he was stepping into, but he adapted to it and found success.

However, his real turning point came at Oracle. The roles there were very process-driven, with little room for creativity or strategic input. Working there felt like he was merely a cog in the machine—completing his part of the process and passing it along. It wasn't fulfilling, and that's when he started thinking, "After all these years of experience, why not leverage my learnings to build something of my own?"

That thought led to the biggest challenge of his career—starting his own venture. It was a bold decision, an opportunity to apply everything that had been learned up to that point and see if it was something he could possibly succeed on his own terms. This is where things got a little heated up. THIS was the ultimate test.

Building Fidrox—A Decade of Growth

Their efforts paid off. They founded Fidrox ten years ago, and from year one, they have been a profitable company. March 2025 marks a decade since they set up the business, and looking back, Raj exudes confidence that it was the right decision.

Today, Fidrox has an impressive client base, including large enterprises, and they have expanded their presence to the US, Europe, and Singapore. One of the most fulfilling aspects of their journey has been their disciplined approach to growth. Instead of taking profits out for personal gains, they reinvested every earning back into the company. That financial discipline has been the cornerstone of their success, allowing them to scale steadily without relying on external funding.

Like any new business, they faced two primary challenges at the outset—securing investments and onboarding their first customers. However, Raj believes the latter is far more critical. Once you have a customer, everything else—including investments—will eventually fall into place.

Many entrepreneurs start by focusing on raising capital, believing they need a perfect setup with an office, infrastructure, and funds before launching. Fidrox took a different approach. When they started in 2015, they didn't even have an office. Their priority was identifying a clear value proposition for potential clients. This proposition was based on their in-depth research, which helped them understand where they could create tangible value for businesses. Their unique selling point was their ability to provide cost-effective and innovative solutions to complex business problems. When they found a customer who recognized this value, they knew they were on the right track.

In fact, they registered the company only after securing their first client. At that time, they didn't even have a physical office—just an address, which happened to be a friend's car shed. It took them a whole year to be confident enough in their progress before committing to a formal office space. Until then, they operated out of cafés, holding meetings at Café Coffee Days every weekend to discuss strategy, execution, and next steps. It wasn't until May 2016 that they officially moved into a rented office space.

A Customer-First Approach to Growth: Fidrox has always prioritized a customer-first philosophy over an investment-first mindset. From the outset, the company strategically focused on acquiring enterprise clients, recognizing the long-term opportunities they offer for expansion. By delivering additional solutions and services over time, such as personalized customer support and regular updates to their software, this approach ensured steady and sustainable growth.

Unlike many startups that seek venture capital based on projections and market potential, Fidrox was built without external funding. The company did not rely on investor pitches or market-size presentations to raise capital. Instead, its work spoke for itself. Over the past decade, Fidrox has demonstrated that growth is possible without external investors—provided there is strong customer buy-in.

A Decade of Self-Sustained Growth

For the past 10 years, Fidrox has consistently reinvested its earnings back into the business rather than extracting profits for personal gains. This disciplined approach has enabled the company to expand steadily while maintaining financial independence.

Today, Fidrox has grown into a 200-member team with an annual revenue of approximately 100 crore, achieving profitability every year—even during the challenges of the COVID-19 pandemic.

In recent years, the company has received multiple investment offers but has chosen to decline them, as external funding has not been a necessity. However, as Fidrox prepares for significant scaling in the near future, which includes expanding its operations to new markets and developing new products, leadership acknowledges that more considerable expansion may require capital. While investment may be considered in the coming year, the core philosophy remains unchanged: if a business is built on credibility and customer value, investments will follow naturally. Banks, financial institutions, and investors consistently seek ventures with proven value and sustainable models.

Fidrox's journey is one of resilience, strategic growth, and an unwavering commitment to customer success. Their foresight and planning have been truly impressive.

The Turning Point: From Corporate to Entrepreneurship

Raj's decision to embark on an entrepreneurial journey stemmed from a sense of monotony—particularly during his tenure at Oracle. While Oracle was a well-established company, its rigid structures limited creativity and problem-solving opportunities. The organization functioned in a way that minimized dependency on individuals, breaking down roles into small, defined processes to ensure continuity. While this operational model was efficient, it left little room for innovation.

Despite the undeniable advantages of working in multinational corporations—financial stability, job security, and brand recognition—many professionals remained in such roles more out of fear than passion. Several of Raj's colleagues expressed a desire to explore new opportunities but lacked the confidence to take the leap. This realization became a central theme in his book Pursuit of an Identity, particularly in the chapter titled "Breaking the chains of Fear." It celebrates the courage of those who break free from self-imposed limitations and step outside their comfort zones. Raj believes that many capable professionals have the potential to carve out independent paths beyond conventional employment, and his story is a testament to the fact that it is possible.

Entrepreneurship had always been Raj's long-term goal, an opportunity to leverage years of experience to create something valuable. However, transitioning from a leadership role at Siemens, where the credibility of an established brand provided access to resources and funding, to launching a venture from scratch was a formidable challenge. The shift from a secure corporate environment to the unpredictable world of entrepreneurship was a leap of faith, requiring courage and determination.

At Siemens, even new initiatives were taken seriously due to the company's reputation. There were investments available, infrastructure in place, and ample resources to support fresh projects. Entrepreneurship, in contrast, requires building everything independently—securing customers, establishing credibility, and managing risks without the safety net of a corporate ecosystem.

The Wisdom of Experience

Despite the challenges, Raj's decision to venture into entrepreneurship proved to be the right one. Looking back, Fidrox's success is a testament to the belief that with resilience, strategic planning, and a commitment to value creation, sustainable growth is not only possible—it is inevitable. And none of this would have been possible without the invaluable guidance and advice from mentors. Their wisdom and experience played a crucial role in shaping Fidrox's journey.

Throughout his career, Raj has been fortunate enough to have been guided by exceptional mentors—senior board members, industry veterans, and influential leaders from the organizations he worked with. At pivotal moments, their insights proved invaluable, shaping his understanding of business strategy, leadership, and long-term vision. Their wisdom, gained from years of experience, has not only guided Raj but also enlightened him about the nuances of business strategy. Observing their ability to navigate complex challenges, Raj recognized early on that success in entrepreneurship wasn't just about having a great idea or technical expertise—it required the wisdom of those who have walked the walk and can now talk the talk.

When he founded Fidrox, Raj made it a priority to establish a strong advisory board. Beyond the core team of promoters, he brought in a couple of seasoned professionals whose sole role was to provide consultation and guidance. Though these people had no equity in the company, their contributions were instrumental in navigating key decisions, helping avoid pitfalls, and steering the company in the right direction.

Fate had an interesting way of coming full circle—Raj's first employer and mentor, Mr. K Vijayaraghavn would go on to become the Chairman of Fidrox's board. A pioneering entrepreneur, he had built an IT company from the ground up in the 1970s. At a time when most Indian professionals were eager to move to the US in the late 1970s, he did the opposite. Having spent the initial years abroad, he made the unconventional decision to return to India and establish a successful business—one he would eventually scale and sell before retiring.

Given his vast experience in business leadership and board governance, Raj requested him to chair Fidrox's board. With decades of wisdom and expertise, his strategic insights proved invaluable. Though not involved in daily operations, his perspective on risk management, long-term vision, and calculated decision-making helped steer Fidrox through critical junctures. A single conversation with him often provided clarity on challenges that seemed insurmountable. His presence on the advisory board brought more than just experience—it instilled a mindset of resilience and foresight that would shape Fidrox's journey ahead.

Beyond him, Fidrox's board included two other seasoned professionals—one from Bosch and another from Siemens. Each brought a wealth of industry experience, but their value wasn't in resolving technical or operational roadblocks. Their role was far more significant: helping Raj and his leadership team see the bigger picture.

One of the most profound lessons Raj learned from them was that at senior levels, business challenges were rarely just about numbers or technology—they were about people. Decision-making, leadership, and managing teams through uncertainty played a far greater role in a company's success than any product or service it offered. With this understanding, Fidrox's advisors helped shape the company's trajectory for the next three to five years, identifying potential pitfalls and guiding crucial decisions.

The true advantage of having such mentors was their ability to remain detached from the daily grind. While Raj and his co-founders were immersed in execution—juggling operations, client relationships, and growth strategies—the advisors maintained a calm, objective outlook. They could anticipate challenges the team might have missed, offering clarity amid the chaos of scaling a business.

For Fidrox, Raj recalls smiling; the turning point wasn't just forming a strong leadership team—it was securing the first customer. That first deal was the hardest to crack, but it was also the most critical one. It was the moment when vision transformed into reality, marking the true beginning of Fidrox's journey.

Navigating Initial Uncertainties amidst Building the Dream Team

Securing the first customer was a major milestone, but the next challenge was even more formidable—convincing colleagues to leave stable jobs and join a fledgling startup. Many of them were with Siemens, and walking away from the security of a multinational for an uncertain venture required more than just persuasion. However, what worked in Raj's favor was the trust he had cultivated over the years.

Raj firmly believed that leadership wasn't defined by titles but by the consistency of one's character. How a leader conducts themselves throughout their career determines how people respond when their support is needed most. His colleagues had seen firsthand how he treated them in the past, and that credibility played a crucial role in earning their trust. Eventually, they chose to take the leap, believing in the vision of building something from the ground up.

While uncertainty loomed, things started falling into place once the business took shape. Even funding—one of the biggest roadblocks for startups—came through more smoothly than expected. When Raj approached the bank for a working capital loan, they approved it without collateral—an uncommon occurrence, especially in India. The reason? Fidrox had a credible purchase order from an enterprise client, giving financial institutions the confidence to back them.

The early days of entrepreneurship were challenging, but uncertainty was nothing new to Raj. His career had unknowingly prepared him for it, each experience shaping him in ways he only came to realize in hindsight. The challenges were diverse, from financial constraints to operational hurdles, and at the time, these moments felt like isolated challenges—complex yet unrelated—but looking back, he saw how they had all been building up to this one journey.

One such defining period was his time in Germany in the early 2000s. Tasked with setting up a business from scratch, he found himself in a country where he didn't know the language, the market, or a single person. The cultural and business landscape was vastly different from what he was accustomed to. Even within India, communication styles and business etiquette varied from state to state—what worked in Karnataka could carry an entirely different meaning in Uttar Pradesh. Europe was no different; each country had its own way of doing business, and Raj had no choice but to adapt quickly.

What seemed like a daunting challenge at the time turned out to be an invaluable lesson in resilience. Navigating unfamiliar territories, understanding diverse cultures, and earning trust in a foreign business environment—these experiences became the foundation of his ability to build something from the ground up. More importantly, it reinforced a fundamental lesson—success wasn't about having all the answers upfront; it was about the willingness to learn, adapt, and push forward despite uncertainties. This underscores the value of learning and adaptation in entrepreneurship, qualities that Raj has honed over the years. And when the time came to start his own venture, Raj realized he wasn't stepping into the unknown after all. He had been preparing for this all along.

When he embarked on his own entrepreneurial journey, he carried the same mindset with him. At its core, his commitment wasn't just about launching a business—it was about creating something of real value. He knew that if he remained focused, adaptable, and persistent, everything else would eventually fall into place.

Just as he had been fortunate with mentors, Raj's journey was also shaped by key allies—individuals who stood by him, believed in his vision, and played a crucial role in building the business. One of the most significant early allies was a former colleague from Siemens, someone Raj deeply trusted for his domain expertise and operational acumen. Bringing him on board was not just a strategic move but a defining moment. It involved a thorough evaluation of his skills, and it underscored the importance of shared leadership in building a strong organization.

For the first time, Raj had to dilute his stakes—an inevitable yet valuable decision that underscored the importance of shared leadership. It was a testament to his belief that building a strong organization required more than just a singular vision; it needed the right people in the right places.

Today, that ally, who plays a crucial role in strategic planning and decision-making, remains a core pillar of Fidrox's leadership team. They ensure seamless execution and uphold the very principles of excellence and efficiency that the company was founded upon.

From the outset, the organization was built with a structured approach that emphasized decentralization and empowerment, avoiding the pitfalls of a one- or two-person-driven entity. Instead, **champions were identified** for every initiative—individuals who took ownership and drove the vision forward.

Today, the company operates with:

- A **well-defined management structure** with multiple levels.
- A growing **team that operates independently** without the need for micromanagement.
- A culture of **trust and responsibility**, where **hiring decisions, execution, and strategy implementation are led by those who are accountable for results**.

Raj no longer oversees most operational decisions personally, and this shift is as necessary as it is intentional. With the right people in place to lead their respective areas, his role has evolved into that of a facilitator—providing financial and strategic support while focusing on brand-building and long-term growth. His priority is no longer micromanaging daily execution but empowering the right people to drive their respective areas with autonomy and accountability.

Challenges have been a constant at every stage of the journey, and they will continue to emerge as Fidrox grows. Some of the most pressing and ongoing obstacles include managing high working capital needs during expansion, navigating the everyday realities of cash flow management, and ensuring transparency and trust within the team as the company scales. When faced with funding challenges, Raj explored every available market option before pursuing the most viable path. Solving one challenge often leads to a new set of hurdles, but that is simply the nature of business. Progress is not about the absence of obstacles—it is about the ability to navigate them with resilience, adaptability, and a relentless drive to keep moving forward.

But here's the key: Raj has always believed that **how you perceive obstacles determines how you handle them.**

- If you see an issue as an **insurmountable problem**, it will weigh you down.
- If you see it as an **opportunity to find a solution**, you keep moving forward.

Raj firmly believes in **building a culture rooted in trust, transparency, and interdependence.** As Krishna's teachings resonate throughout the scripture of the Bhagavad Gita, *"Interdependence is a higher skill than working independently."* This philosophy directly shapes Raj's approach to leadership.

He emphasizes the importance of empowering the team rather than shouldering everything on his own. "I don't intend to do everything myself," he shares. "I always thought that the key to success was building a team. A team comes with its own good and bad, with its own limitations, but the key is to leverage the strengths of each member and navigate through their limitations. It's an art that I've learned through my work experience."

Raj sees leadership not as a solo endeavor but as a collective journey. He is focused on the long-term vision of the organization while handling short-term challenges with clarity. As each challenge is overcome, the organization grows stronger. For Raj, the journey has been nothing short of exciting, full of growth and discovery.

Every significant challenge brings with it moments of uncertainty—times when solutions aren't immediately apparent. But overcoming these challenges brings an undeniable satisfaction and a sense of forward momentum. This sense of achievement comes not only from navigating the hurdles but also from ensuring that those around him are recognized and valued for their contributions.

At an organizational level, Raj has worked to build a culture of reward and recognition at every level. When someone makes a meaningful contribution—especially during moments of uncertainty or crisis—their efforts are:

- **Recognized publicly** in front of the entire team.
- **Appreciated** during company events as formal acknowledgment.
- **Rewarded**, not necessarily with grand prizes, but through meaningful gestures of appreciation.

This approach has become a key motivator within the team. Raj has learned that people value acknowledgment more than material rewards, and this system has helped create a culture where effort, resilience, and problem-solving are genuinely appreciated.

Ultimately, Raj believes that the greatest reward is the satisfaction of knowing that the team, as a unit, has moved forward, no matter how challenging the path may have been. Success, for Raj, has never been about personal accolades or dramatic transformations. It has always been about collective progress—ensuring that every challenge faced becomes an opportunity for the team to grow stronger. While finance and investments fall under his direct responsibilities, many other challenges are tackled by his team. Recognizing and appreciating their contributions has helped foster a culture of trust, collaboration, and problem-solving.

Yet, at the heart of it all, Raj remains deeply grounded. His life has always been rooted in simplicity and sustainability, and professional achievements have never altered that foundation.

For Raj, the key to sustainable success lies in consistency—remaining true to oneself while evolving professionally. If one creates two separate versions of life—one for success and another for an "ordinary" existence—it leads to an imbalance. Instead, he believes in building a life that remains steady, regardless of professional highs and lows.

Ultimately, leadership is not about doing everything alone; it is about empowering others, navigating challenges as a team, and staying true to one's core values. And that, more than anything, is what defines Raj's journey.

RAJ GOPAL, CO-AUTHOR

Raj Gopal is an entrepreneur with over thirty years of experience in the ICT industry. As the Founder and CEO of Fidrox Technologies, he has helped many individuals achieve their holistic goals, which include both professional and personal aspects.

Raj is passionate about entrepreneurship, personal development, and other related topics. He enjoys helping others realize their potential through practical strategies and personal insight. His exposure to a wide spectrum of industries enables him to connect with people and opportunities.

ABOUT THE AUTHORS

This is a book written by industry experts, each contributing a chapter. Here's a list of all the CO-AUTHORS of this publication (in no particular order):

- Murali Dharan
- John Cherian
- Philip Samuel
- Mahendra Patel
- Anil Nair
- Yadavalli Subramanyam
- Dr. Venkataramana
- Atma Gunupudi
- Raj Gopal

Published by: Raam Anand